We Will Not Be Ruled

A People's Handbook for Democratic Resistance

We Will Not Be Ruled

A People's Handbook for Democratic Resistance

We Will Not Be Ruled:
A People's Handbook for Democratic Resistance

Richard Rawson, Psy.D., MBA

© 2025 Richard Rawson
All rights reserved.

No part of this book may be reproduced, stored, or transmitted in any form or by any means without the prior written permission of the author, except for brief quotations used in reviews or scholarly works.

This book is intended for educational and informational purposes only. It does not constitute legal, political, or professional advice.

ISBN: 979-8-9878416-8-6

Published by Rawson Internet Marketing.
United States of America.

On Democratic Endurance

Democracy is rarely sustained by moments of outrage or heroic resistance. It endures through ordinary participation carried forward over time.

We Will Not Be Ruled explores how democratic responsibility can be practiced without exhaustion, moral pressure, or permanent crisis. Rather than focusing only on threats or decline, the book examines how engagement becomes sustainable—how people contribute consistently, step back when necessary, and return without abandoning responsibility.

This is a guide to democratic endurance: participation designed to coexist with work, family, disagreement, and fatigue—and to last beyond any single moment of alarm.

Table of Contents

Chapter 1: Why Democracy Is Under Threat 1

Chapter 2: Learning From Failed Resistance 15

Chapter 3: The Authoritarian Playbook 27

Chapter 4: Breaking The Authoritarian Spell 41

Chapter 5: Creating Democratic Solidarity 53

Chapter 6: Winning Hearts And Minds 65

Chapter 7: The Economic Battlefield 79

Chapter 8: Converting The Passive Enablers 93

Chapter 9: Activating The Disengaged 109

Chapter 10: Local Power Building 123

Chapter 11: Measuring And Building Victory 137

CHAPTER 1
Why Democracy Is Under Threat

Section 1

How Democracy Slips Away

When democratic systems begin to erode, the first signs are rarely dramatic. There are no tanks in the streets, no sudden suspension of elections. Instead, the changes arrive through announcements that sound technical and procedural—adjustments framed as reforms, efficiency measures, or routine updates.

On paper, these changes often appear minor, even boring. Their effects are not. They weaken opposition voices, narrow accountability, and shift the balance of power—not through spectacle or force, but through legal language, administrative discretion, and decisions made quietly behind closed doors. Their success depends less on enthusiasm than on passive cooperation.

This is how democracy disappears in the modern era. Not through coups or soldiers in the streets, and rarely overnight. It erodes gradually, often under the cover of legality and normal procedure.

Versions of this pattern have played out repeatedly over the past several decades, across very different political and cultural contexts. Countries as varied as Hungary, Poland, Turkey, Venezuela, the Philippines, Brazil, and even long-established democracies have experienced similar forms of erosion.

Institutions weaken slowly. Citizens reassure themselves that courts will intervene, that elections will correct the course, that someone, somewhere, will step in before the damage becomes irreversible. By the time the shift is undeniable, much of the democratic infrastructure that once made resistance possible has already been compromised.

When people look back, they often ask the same questions. *How did this happen so easily? And why did so few resist until it was too late?*

One of the most important truths authoritarian movements work to conceal is that they are not, and have never been, the majority. This fact matters more than almost anything else in the effort to defend democratic systems.

The most dangerous claim authoritarian leaders make is that they represent "the people" as a single, unified mass demanding strong leadership and decisive control. That claim serves a strategic purpose. It creates an illusion of inevitability, making resistance feel naïve or futile. It convinces people that opposition is isolated, marginal, or already defeated.

The empirical reality looks very different. Across countries and political systems, the core authoritarian base rarely exceeds a small fraction of the population. Even at moments of peak influence, it is typically closer to one-fifth than to a true majority.

In practical terms, this means that in any given group, only a minority would actively choose authoritarian rule if presented clearly with what it entails: the dismantling of checks and balances, the concentration of power, the suppression of dissent, and the erosion of equal protection under the law.

Yet again and again, this minority succeeds in reshaping entire societies. It does so not through numbers, but through conditions. Democracy depends on participation, while authoritarianism thrives on passivity.

Democratic systems require engagement, cooperation across difference, and a willingness to act collectively. Authoritarian systems exploit hesitation, withdrawal, and fragmentation, often encouraging people to retreat into private life or to rationalize erosion as temporary, tolerable, or unavoidable.

This dynamic represents democracy's central vulnerability. Authoritarians do not take power alone. They rely on silence, rationalization, and the quiet decisions of people who look away, who tell themselves that the situation is not ideal but not intolerable, or who believe that such outcomes cannot happen where they live. Understanding how a minority can win without majority support is foundational to everything that follows in this book.

Once this structure becomes visible, the sense of inevitability begins to dissolve.

What appears to be unstoppable momentum reveals itself as something far more fragile: a system sustained only as long as enough people continue to disengage. Recognizing that fragility is the first step toward interrupting it.

Section 2

The Four Groups in This Fight

To understand how a minority can reshape an entire society, it helps to look more closely at how people actually respond when democracy comes under pressure. Populations do not divide cleanly into "good" and "bad," or "democratic" and "authoritarian." Instead, they tend to sort themselves into roles. These roles appear with remarkable consistency across countries, cultures, and political systems, and they do more than describe attitudes. They determine whether democratic erosion accelerates or stalls.

Most people have encountered these roles in everyday life, even if they have never named them. Think of the last family gathering where politics surfaced unexpectedly. Someone praises strong leadership and dismisses concerns about norms. Someone else shifts the conversation, uncomfortable but unwilling to engage. Another person shrugs and says they no longer follow politics at all. And perhaps someone tries, awkwardly, to explain why institutions and rules matter. That moment is not just an uncomfortable social interaction. It is a small-scale reflection of how democratic systems fracture under pressure.

When democratic norms begin to erode, societies reliably divide into four groups.

The first is the authoritarian base. This group typically makes up about one-fifth of the population. These are the true believers. They do not merely tolerate authoritarianism; they actively want it. They are drawn to strong, dominant leaders who promise certainty in uncertain times and who frame complexity as weakness. For them, democracy often feels chaotic, inefficient, and indecisive. Compromise looks like failure, pluralism like decay, and limits on power like unnecessary obstacles.

What matters most about this group is not just what they believe, but how firmly they believe it. Their attachment to authoritarian leadership is not primarily driven by policy preferences. It is emotional and identity-based. Evidence and counterarguments rarely move them, because facts are not what bind them to strongman politics in the first place. At the same time, this group cannot win on its own. Its numbers are too small to reshape a society without assistance.

That assistance comes from the second group: the passive enablers. This is often the most consequential group in any democracy under threat, and it usually represents roughly thirty percent of the population. Passive enablers do not see themselves as authoritarian. Many are uneasy about norm-breaking behavior, inflammatory rhetoric, or the concentration of power. But they rationalize what they see. They tell themselves that the leader's style is unfortunate but effective, that the alternatives would be worse, or that politics has always been corrupt anyway. They urge patience, restraint, or simply giving things time.

What defines this group is not enthusiasm, but accommodation. Passive enablers prioritize stability, personal security, and short-term benefits over democratic principles. They minimize warning signs and normalize behavior that would once have triggered alarm. In doing so, they provide something authoritarians desperately need: social license. Unlike the authoritarian base, passive enablers are persuadable. They often experience discomfort and cognitive dissonance. But unless that tension is activated—unless the real costs of accommodation become visible and unavoidable—they continue to enable consolidation of power. Without them, authoritarian movements stall. With them, minorities can plausibly claim to speak for "the people."

The third group is the disengaged, which also tends to make up around thirty percent of the population. These are the people who withdraw entirely from political life. They express cynicism rather than allegiance, insisting that all sides are corrupt, that nothing ever changes, or that politics has little relevance to their daily struggles. Many are focused on survival, not civic engagement, and for good reason. Economic insecurity, inequality, and repeated institutional failure have taught them that participation often feels futile.

It is important to recognize that disengagement is frequently rational. Many people in this group have been promised representation and delivered disappointment. But in a democracy under threat, disengagement is not neutral. It functions as permission. When large numbers of people stop paying attention, stop participating, and stop believing their actions matter, the barriers to authoritarian consolidation fall away quietly. Like the passive enablers, the disengaged are persuadable, but not through fear, shame, or abstract appeals to civic duty. What moves them is evidence that engagement can produce tangible results and that democracy can function as a practical tool rather than an empty ritual.

The final group consists of pro-democracy defenders, usually about twenty percent of the population. These are the people who show up when voting rights are threatened, who support independent media, who run for local office when extremists target school boards, and who have conversations others avoid. They do not simply believe in democracy; they practice it, even when doing so carries personal cost. They tend to have high democratic efficacy and a strong sense that their actions matter.

Like the authoritarian base, this group is relatively stable in size. They are unlikely to abandon their commitment. But they face a hard limitation. On their own, they can only hold the line. They cannot secure democracy by themselves.

This leads to the basic arithmetic that underlies everything that follows. Roughly twenty percent form the authoritarian base. About thirty percent function as passive enablers. Another thirty percent are disengaged. And around twenty percent actively defend democratic norms. The middle sixty percent—the enablers and the disengaged—constitute the true battlefield. Authoritarian movements succeed only when that middle continues to accommodate or withdraw. When accommodation turns into resistance, or when disengagement shifts toward participation, the balance changes quickly and dramatically.

This is not idealism. It is arithmetic. And it points to a critical conclusion. The decisive work of democratic defense does not lie in converting committed authoritarians or preaching to those already engaged. It lies in activating the middle. Understanding these four groups strips away the illusion of inevitability and exposes the fundamental weakness of authoritarian movements. They cannot win without help, and what has been given—silence, normalization, and withdrawal—can also be withdrawn.

In the next section, we'll examine how authoritarians exploit this structure deliberately, using fear, institutional weakness, and exhaustion to keep the middle from moving. Because once the mechanics are visible, interruption becomes possible.

Section 3

How Authoritarians Win Without Numbers

At first glance, the numbers should be reassuring. If only a small minority actively supports authoritarian rule, democracy ought to prevail. A determined few should not be able to overpower a reluctant majority. Yet history repeatedly tells a different story. Again and again, minorities succeed in capturing democratic systems—not because most people want authoritarianism, but because authoritarians understand something essential about how power actually works.

They do not need to persuade everyone, or even most people. What they need is to shape the environment in which everyone else makes decisions.

Modern authoritarians rarely announce themselves as dictators. They do not suspend elections outright or abolish constitutions in a single dramatic act. Instead, they hollow democratic systems from the inside, preserving their outward appearance while steadily removing their substance. Institutions continue to exist, procedures remain in place, and the language of democracy is carefully maintained. What changes is how those elements function in practice.

Authoritarian movements achieve this without numbers by relying on three interconnected strategies: fear, the exploitation of democratic weakness, and exhaustion. Taken together, these strategies allow a minority to govern a society that never explicitly chose authoritarian rule.

The first strategy is fear. Authoritarian movements depend on a constant sense of threat. Sometimes those threats are grounded in reality—crime, economic instability, or rapid social change. More often, they are exaggerated, distorted, or deliberately manufactured. Immigrants are framed as invaders, political opponents as enemies, journalists as traitors, and minority groups as existential dangers. The specific target matters less than the psychological effect. Fear narrows thinking, reduces tolerance for complexity, and encourages people to trade freedom for the promise of safety.

When fear becomes chronic rather than episodic, democratic restraint begins to look irresponsible. People stop asking whether extraordinary measures are justified and start asking why they are not happening faster. Authoritarian leaders present themselves as the only ones willing to act decisively, framing democratic norms as weaknesses that leave the nation exposed. Importantly, fear does not need to convince everyone. It only needs to keep passive enablers anxious and disengaged citizens overwhelmed.

The second strategy involves exploiting the internal tensions of democracy itself. Democratic systems are built on principles that can be turned against them when interpreted in bad faith. Freedom of speech can be weaponized through disinformation. Majority rule can be used to undermine minority rights. Electoral legitimacy can be invoked to override constitutional limits. Tolerance can be exploited by those who have no intention of tolerating opposition.

Rather than openly breaking democratic rules, modern authoritarians rewrite them. Procedures are adjusted, qualifications redefined, institutions restructured, and norms quietly reinterpreted. Each change appears technical, defensible, and often legal when viewed in isolation. Taken together, however, these shifts steadily concentrate power while preserving democratic appearances. This is why democratic erosion often remains invisible until it is well advanced. Most people do not track judicial appointment rules, regulatory changes, or administrative restructurings. By the time outcomes clearly change—when courts no longer constrain power or elections no longer offer meaningful choice—the architecture that once protected democracy has already been dismantled.

The third strategy is exhaustion, and it is often the most underestimated.

Authoritarian systems generate chaos not to confuse indefinitely, but to wear people down. Rules change constantly, scandals overlap, contradictions multiply, and crises never fully resolve. Attention is pulled in too many directions at once. Over time, people become not just physically tired, but cognitively and emotionally depleted.

When everything feels urgent, nothing feels actionable. Reflection gives way to reaction, and eventually even reaction feels futile. People stop asking whether something is right or wrong and begin asking whether it is worth the effort to care at all. This is where resignation sets in. The belief that nothing can be done, that power is already entrenched, or that resistance is pointless becomes self-reinforcing. Authoritarian systems do not need mass repression if enough people decide that engagement is no longer worth the cost. Silence and withdrawal do the work for them.

Together, these strategies produce a predictable pattern. An electoral victory, often without a true majority, is followed by rapid consolidation of key institutions. Rules are adjusted to favor incumbents. Information environments are shaped. Civil society faces pressure. Economic relationships reward compliance and punish resistance. From the outside, the system still looks democratic. Elections occur, courts exist, and media operates. From the inside, however, power no longer meaningfully changes hands, accountability weakens, and choice becomes increasingly symbolic.

Because this transformation happens gradually, many people recognize it only when reversing it becomes extraordinarily difficult. That brings us to a deeper question. If authoritarianism depends on fear, institutional weakness, and exhaustion, why do so many ordinary, well-intentioned people go along with it? Why do people who value democracy remain silent as it erodes?

The answer is not found in ideology or ignorance alone. To understand it, we have to look inward. In the next section, we'll examine the psychology of looking away and the quiet mechanisms that turn decent people into enablers of systems they never explicitly chose.

Section 4

Why Good People Enable Bad Systems

When democratic systems begin to erode, the most unsettling question is not why extremists push them. It is why so many ordinary people go along. Not zealots or true believers, but neighbors, colleagues, friends, and family members—people who value decency and who would sincerely say that they believe in democracy. History points to an uncomfortable but consistent pattern. Authoritarian systems do not survive on fanaticism alone. They survive on accommodation, and that accommodation rarely begins as a moral choice. It begins as a psychological one.

Most people do not wake up one day and decide to abandon democratic values. What they experience instead is pressure: pressure to manage daily life, pressure to avoid conflict, pressure to protect their family, their job, and their sense of normalcy. When early warning signs appear, the mind looks for ways to reduce discomfort. *This probably isn't as serious as it sounds. Someone else will handle it. Institutions exist for a reason. It can't really happen here.* These thoughts are not signs of bad character. They are common human responses to uncertainty and threat.

Psychologists describe this pattern as normalcy bias, the tendency to assume that tomorrow will resemble today even when evidence suggests otherwise. It is a coping mechanism. If the mind fully absorbed every potential danger at once, it would freeze. Instead, it narrows attention, minimizes risk, and delays judgment. In ordinary circumstances, this strategy is adaptive. In periods of democratic erosion, it becomes dangerous.

A related force is responsibility diffusion. When problems feel large and systemic, individuals assume that someone else is better positioned to act. Courts will intervene. Journalists will expose wrongdoing. Political leaders will step in. Each person waits for confirmation that action is truly necessary, and by the time that confirmation arrives, the cost of acting has increased. This is not apathy. It is uncertainty combined with social hesitation. The result, however, is the same. When everyone waits, nothing happens, and silence—however unintentional—creates space for momentum to continue.

Comfort also plays a role, and this is harder to acknowledge. Many people living through democratic backsliding are not immediately harmed by it. Some benefit, at least temporarily. Their job remains stable, their neighborhood feels secure, their taxes are lower, or their values seem affirmed. As a result, the erosion of democratic norms feels abstract. It becomes something to worry about later rather than something that demands immediate response. Small compromises begin to feel reasonable. These rationalizations do not feel like surrender. They feel like pragmatism. Over time, pragmatism hardens into habit.

At this point, it becomes important to name a difficult truth. Silence is not neutral. In systems under stress, silence functions as permission—not because people intend harm, but because systems respond to behavior rather than intention. When violations go unchallenged, they normalize. When norms break without consequence, they weaken. When enough people adapt, adaptation becomes the baseline. This is how extraordinary measures become routine without ever feeling extraordinary in the moment.

Fear of loss further reinforces this dynamic. Speaking up carries risk: risk to employment, reputation, relationships, and in some cases personal safety. The benefits of resistance, meanwhile, are uncertain. People wonder whether their actions will matter, whether they will be isolated, or whether they will simply make things worse. Often without conscious calculation, many conclude that staying quiet feels safer than acting. Not because they approve of what is happening, but because they doubt their own efficacy. This is how good people become enablers without ever seeing themselves that way.

The tragedy is that these choices are usually made individually, while their consequences are collective. Each person believes their silence is insignificant. Each compromise feels small and temporary. But together, they accumulate. Not into a single dramatic collapse, but into a gradual surrender.

History is unforgiving in retrospect. Looking back, it seems obvious what should have been done and when. We ask why people did not act sooner or more decisively. What history rarely captures is how unclear things felt in real time, how costly action appeared, and how exhausting constant vigilance became. The danger is not that people stop caring. It is that caring becomes too heavy to carry alone.

This points toward a crucial shift in how democratic defense must be understood. It cannot rely on individual moral heroism. It has to reduce the cost of participation, make action visible, and replace isolation with shared effort. People are far more willing to act when they know they are not acting alone. The solution to silence is not guilt or condemnation. It is structure: support, coordination, clear roles, and shared responsibility. When resistance becomes collective, courage becomes more accessible.

If this chapter has done its work, it should leave you with clarity rather than despair. Authoritarian movements are minorities. They rely on fear, institutional weakness, and exhaustion. They advance through accommodation more often than force. Which means their greatest vulnerability is not ideology, but withdrawal. And what has been withdrawn—attention, participation, responsibility—can also be restored.

In the next chapter, we turn to why past resistance movements, often sincere and deeply committed, failed to halt democratic erosion. Not to assign blame, but to learn how resistance can become durable rather than reactive. Because defending democracy is not about purity. It is about persistence.

CHAPTER 2
Learning From Failed Resistance

Section 1

When Resistance Flares and Fades

The air felt electric with possibility. In a small public square just blocks from Wall Street, thousands gathered around a makeshift encampment that had become the unlikely center of a global movement. Handwritten signs demanded accountability from financial elites. Working groups formed spontaneously to handle food, media, medical care, and legal support. When someone spoke, the crowd echoed their words back, sentence by sentence, through what became known as the People's Mic.

For a brief moment in the fall of 2011, it felt as though something real was happening. Occupy Wall Street had captured global attention. *We are the ninety-nine percent* gave language to a shared sense of injustice that had been building for decades. Economic inequality, long treated as background noise, suddenly became unavoidable. For a moment that felt almost breathtaking, it seemed possible that a popular uprising might force meaningful change.

And then it faded.

Not in a dramatic collapse. Not with a decisive defeat. But quietly. What remained were a slogan, scattered memories, and a lingering question: *what happened?*

The pattern should feel familiar. Massive protests erupt with moral clarity and extraordinary energy. They dominate headlines, flood public spaces, and feel unstoppable. Then, slowly or suddenly, they dissipate. Institutions remain largely intact. Power adapts and moves on. New movements rise, and the cycle repeats.

The question is not whether protest matters. It does. The question is why so many movements that feel powerful fail to become powerful in reality.

To understand what separates resistance that lasts from resistance that fades, we have to stop treating failure as taboo. Not to assign blame, diminish courage, or rewrite history with cynicism—but to learn. When movements repeat the same patterns while expecting different outcomes, they burn enormous energy without producing durable change. In an era of accelerating authoritarian pressure, that is not a luxury democracy can afford.

This chapter looks directly at three major resistance efforts that fell short of their potential: Occupy Wall Street, the wave of mass protests that followed a destabilizing political transition, and the Women's March. Each mobilized millions. Each reshaped public conversation. Each inspired deep commitment and sacrifice. And each struggled to translate visibility into lasting power.

The goal here is not to label these movements failures. It is to understand how and why their impact stalled, so future resistance can be built differently. Effective resistance is not just about showing up. It is about what happens after the crowd disperses.

We begin with Occupy Wall Street, not because it lacked vision, but because it exposed a tension that continues to haunt progressive movements: the tension between democracy and organization, between participation and strategy, between rejecting hierarchy and building power. Occupy did not falter because people stopped caring. It faltered because it never resolved how a movement without leaders could confront institutions built on leadership, coordination, and endurance.

Understanding that failure clearly and honestly is the first step toward doing better.

Section 2

Why Occupy Wall Street Lost Momentum

Occupy Wall Street did not lose momentum because people stopped believing in its message. In many ways, the opposite was true. Public support for the core idea behind Occupy—the critique of extreme inequality and unaccountable financial power—remained strong long after the encampments disappeared. The problem was not belief. It was structure.

From the beginning, Occupy defined itself by what it refused to become. There would be no formal leaders, no centralized authority, no hierarchy, and no demands negotiated behind closed doors. These choices were deliberate and principled. Many participants had lived through political systems that concentrated power, excluded voices, and made decisions far removed from those affected by them. Occupy was, in part, a rejection of that entire model.

The movement did not simply oppose economic injustice. It attempted to embody a different way of organizing society. That aspiration mattered. But it also created a dilemma Occupy never fully resolved.

Horizontal organization—where decisions are made collectively and authority is deliberately flattened—can be powerful in the early stages of a movement. It builds trust, invites participation, and resists domination. People feel ownership because they genuinely have it. As a movement grows, however, the demands of coordination increase. More people bring more viewpoints. More viewpoints require longer deliberation. Longer deliberation slows response.

What once feels inclusive can begin to feel immobilizing.

At Occupy assemblies, decisions often required consensus or near-consensus. In theory, this protected fairness. In practice, it allowed a small number of participants to delay or block action indefinitely. Meetings stretched for hours. Energy drained. Urgent decisions stalled. While participants debated process, conditions outside the encampments kept changing. Media attention shifted. Public patience waned. Authorities adjusted their tactics. Occupy, committed to remaining leaderless, had no mechanism for rapid strategic response.

This was not a failure of intelligence or commitment. It was a mismatch between values and environment.

Modern power structures—corporate, political, and media—operate hierarchically. They move quickly, coordinate across institutions, and reward decisiveness. A movement that refuses all hierarchy is effectively choosing to compete under different rules. That choice has consequences.

Without designated leadership, no one could speak for the movement in sustained negotiations. Without delegated authority, responsibility diffused. When problems arose, there was no clear mechanism for course correction. Without a shared strategy, tactics multiplied without coherence. Some participants prioritized disruption. Others focused on mutual aid. Some pursued policy reform, while others rejected policy engagement entirely.

None of these goals were illegitimate. But without a framework to integrate them, they pulled the movement in competing directions.

There is a common misconception that Occupy failed because it lacked demands. That explanation is too simple. The deeper issue was the absence of a decision-making structure capable of translating moral clarity into durable power. Democracy inside a movement does not automatically produce effectiveness outside it. Participation alone does not substitute for strategy. Rejecting hierarchy does not eliminate power; it leaves it unorganized.

As weeks turned into months, exhaustion set in. Maintaining encampments required constant labor. Internal conflicts intensified. Security concerns grew. Legal pressure mounted. Authorities, meanwhile, learned how to respond. They coordinated evictions across cities, framed the movement as impractical and disorganized, and waited.

Eventually, the physical spaces that sustained Occupy were dismantled. Without those spaces, the movement struggled to reconstitute itself—not because people stopped caring, but because there was no infrastructure to carry momentum forward.

Occupy revealed something essential about modern resistance. Movements that prioritize participation over coordination can mobilize enormous energy, but they struggle to sustain it. Movements that reject leadership entirely avoid certain dangers, but they create others.

The lesson is not that Occupy should have been more authoritarian. It is that durable resistance requires intentional structure—structure that preserves participation while enabling strategy, distributes authority without dissolving responsibility, and adapts under pressure. Without that, even the most compelling moral critique can fade without producing lasting institutional change.

None of this diminishes what Occupy achieved. It reshaped public discourse, changed how inequality was discussed, and inspired a generation of activists. But inspiration is not the same as power. And power—durable, defensive power—is what democracies under threat ultimately require.

In the next section, we'll turn to a different kind of failure—not a failure of organization, but a failure of focus. We'll examine the mass protests that followed a polarizing presidential election, and why numbers alone were not enough to halt democratic erosion.

Section 3

When Mass Protest Isn't Enough

In January of 2017, millions of people poured into the streets. They gathered the day after a presidential inauguration that many experienced as a profound shock—not only politically, but morally. Across cities in the United States and around the world, crowds assembled in unprecedented numbers.

It was one of the largest protest mobilizations in modern history.

The message was unmistakable. Resistance was real. Opposition was widespread. Authoritarian impulses would not go unchallenged. And yet, four years later, democratic institutions were weaker, not stronger.

How does a movement with such extraordinary numbers fail to produce lasting defensive power?

The problem was not commitment. People marched in freezing weather. They took time off work. They donated, organized locally, and stayed engaged for years. The problem was that mass protest, by itself, does not equal leverage. Visibility is not the same as influence. Numbers are not the same as power. Expression is not the same as constraint.

Authoritarian-leaning systems can absorb enormous public anger, so long as that anger does not translate into mechanisms that limit their freedom to act.

Large protests serve several vital functions. They signal dissent. They reduce isolation. They shift public narratives. They energize participants. But they also have structural limits. A protest occurs at a moment in time. Institutions operate continuously.

Once the march ends, the system resumes its work. Legislation advances. Appointments are made. Rules are rewritten. Norms erode. Unless protest is connected to sustained pressure points—electoral consequences, legal challenges, economic costs, or institutional disruption—it remains symbolic rather than constraining.

In the years that followed that election, protests were massive but diffuse. They lacked a shared strategic objective beyond expressing opposition. Different groups focused on different threats: immigration policy, judicial appointments, environmental regulation, civil rights, media integrity. Each concern was legitimate.

But without integration, they competed for attention and energy.

Because protests were not anchored to specific institutional choke points, those in power learned they could wait them out. Crowds eventually go home. Terms continue.

There was also a mismatch in timing. Protests tend to surge in response to acute events—an election, a court ruling, a scandal. Authoritarian consolidation unfolds gradually. It advances through appointments rather than coups, through procedural changes rather than dramatic ruptures, through normalization rather than shock.

Mass protest excels at responding to moments. It struggles to sustain pressure across years of incremental change.

There is also a psychological trap. When millions show up, participants often feel that something decisive has already occurred. The presence of so many others creates a sense of completion. *We've spoken. We've been heard. Surely this will matter.*

But institutions do not respond to sentiment. They respond to incentives and constraints. If those do not change, behavior does not change.

None of this means the protests were meaningless. They mattered deeply to those who participated. They reshaped how people understood one another. They created networks that later became organizing hubs.

But as defensive tools, they were incomplete. They lacked follow-through structures capable of translating outrage into institutional limits.

This reveals a difficult but necessary distinction. Resistance that feels powerful is not always resistance that is powerful. Power is measured by what it prevents. *Does it stop harmful policy? Block illegitimate appointments? Impose costs on norm-breaking behavior? Change the strategic calculations of those in authority?*

If the answer is no, resistance—however morally compelling—remains vulnerable to being ignored.

Authoritarian-leaning leaders understand this dynamic well. They tolerate protest as long as it remains expressive rather than coercive. They allow demonstrations that burn energy without imposing consequences. In some cases, they even benefit from it, using protest as evidence of disorder, instability, or elite hysteria.

When resistance remains confined to spectacle, it becomes manageable.

The lesson here is not that mass protest should be abandoned. It is that protest must be embedded within a broader strategy—one that links expression to leverage, visibility to constraint, and numbers to durability.

Without that linkage, even the largest mobilizations risk becoming rituals of dissent: emotionally sustaining, morally affirming, and politically insufficient.

In the next section, we'll examine a final case study: the Women's March—a movement that combined scale, moral clarity, and organizational ambition, yet still struggled to convert momentum into lasting institutional defense. Understanding why brings us closer to what effective resistance actually requires.

Section 4

Why the Women's March Lost Momentum

In January of two thousand seventeen, the Women's March brought millions into the streets. It was vast, emotional, and unmistakably visible. Across cities and continents, people gathered to reject misogyny, authoritarian rhetoric, and the rollback of hard-won rights. The scale was historic, and for many participants it was the first protest they had ever attended. For a moment, it felt like the beginning of something enduring.

Unlike Occupy Wall Street, the Women's March did not reject organization outright. It had recognized leaders, access to funding, national visibility, and partnerships with established advocacy groups. In other words, it possessed many of the structural elements Occupy lacked. And yet, despite these advantages, its long-term political impact fell short of its early promise. Understanding why requires examining a different failure mode—not a lack of structure, but a lack of strategic focus.

From the beginning, the Women's March attempted to carry an exceptionally broad set of causes. Reproductive rights, racial justice, immigration reform, economic inequality, LGBTQ+ rights, environmental protection, and opposition to authoritarian leadership were all placed under the same banner. Each concern was legitimate, and each constituency deserved attention. But taken together, they produced a movement without a clear center of gravity. When a movement tries to stand for everything at once, it often struggles to prioritize anything effectively.

This lack of prioritization had practical consequences. Energy dispersed across dozens of issues, while opponents concentrated narrowly on consolidating power through appointments, procedural changes, and institutional capture. Resistance spoke in many voices and directions, while authority acted with singular purpose. The asymmetry mattered, because political power rewards focus far more consistently than it rewards breadth.

There was also a persistent tension between coalition-building and coherence. Broad coalitions are essential for democratic defense; they expand reach, legitimacy, and resilience. But coalitions require ongoing maintenance. Disagreements must be negotiated, conflicts managed, and trade-offs made explicit. When these processes are avoided—or postponed in the name of unity—fractures still emerge, often publicly and destructively. Over time, internal disputes within the Women's March leadership drew attention away from external threats. Media narratives shifted, public trust eroded, and momentum slowed. None of this negated the sincerity or importance of the movement, but it weakened its ability to function as a sustained defensive force.

Another challenge was the gap between mobilization and institution-building. The Women's March excelled at bringing people into public space, but it struggled to keep participants engaged in less visible, longer-term work. Voting infrastructure, candidate recruitment, local organizing, legal defense, and administrative oversight lack the emotional payoff of mass demonstration. They are slower, less affirming, and more tedious. Yet these are precisely the arenas where democratic defense is won or lost. Without clear pathways from protest to participation, many supporters gradually disengaged—not because they stopped caring, but because they could not see where their effort would matter most.

Taken together, the Women's March illustrates a different lesson than Occupy Wall Street or the post-election protests. It shows that scale and structure alone are not enough. Without strategic prioritization, movements risk becoming permanent expressions of concern rather than engines of constraint. They inspire, affirm, and connect, but they do not necessarily limit power.

Learning From Failed Resistance

At this point, a pattern becomes clear. Occupy Wall Street revealed the limits of participation without coordination. Mass post-election protests revealed the limits of numbers without leverage. The Women's March revealed the limits of breadth without focus. Each movement exposed a different vulnerability, and together they point toward a deeper conclusion.

Effective resistance is not spontaneous. It is designed. It requires deliberate choices—sometimes uncomfortable ones—about where to focus, how to allocate energy, and which battles matter most. It requires saying not now to some causes in order to defend the system that makes all causes possible. And it requires moving beyond the emotional satisfaction of protest toward the quieter discipline of power-building.

This does not mean these movements failed in any absolute sense. They changed lives, reshaped public consciousness, and laid groundwork future efforts will build upon. But they also show what democratic defense cannot rely on alone: passion without structure, visibility without leverage, and breadth without strategy.

Chapter 2 has asked you to sit with failure—not to diminish courage, but to extract clarity. Because when resistance repeats familiar patterns while expecting different outcomes, democratic erosion continues quietly and effectively. The point of this examination is not to discourage action. It is to sharpen it. Before resistance can be redesigned, it has to understand what it is up against—not just in theory, but in practice.

In the next chapter, we turn our attention to that reality. Not to movements that failed, but to the systems that succeeded. We examine the modern authoritarian playbook: how democratic erosion actually unfolds, why it so often outpaces resistance, and how power consolidates without open confrontation. Because effective resistance begins not with urgency, but with recognition. You cannot interrupt a strategy you do not yet see.

CHAPTER 3
The Authoritarian Playbook

WE WILL NOT BE RULED

Section 1

It Doesn't Arrive the Way You Expect

Most people imagine authoritarianism arriving with force—uniforms, soldiers, curfews, a sudden rupture with the past. That image is comforting because it makes authoritarianism easy to recognize. It is also dangerously misleading.

Modern authoritarianism rarely arrives through open violence. It arrives through procedures, legal language, personnel changes, and reforms that sound technical or temporary. It advances slowly enough that many people do not notice it happening at all.

Sally Yates had spent nearly three decades inside the Department of Justice. She served under Republican administrations and Democratic ones, doing what career civil servants are meant to do: apply the law as it exists, not as political leaders wish it to be. When a new administration took office in 2017, she expected turbulence. Every transition brings it. What she did not expect was how quickly loyalty would replace legality as the governing standard.

When Yates instructed Justice Department lawyers not to defend an executive order she believed was unconstitutional, she was fired within days. That decision made headlines. What mattered more was what followed. Career officials resigned. Others were sidelined. Safeguards that had protected independent judgment were quietly dismantled—not chaotically or impulsively, but methodically.

One former Justice Department official later described it this way: *"The scariest part wasn't the abuses themselves. It was how deliberately they identified which rules mattered—and then removed them, one by one."*

This is the part many people miss. Authoritarianism today is rarely reckless. It is careful.

Modern authoritarians do not seize institutions; they inhabit them. They do not abolish courts; they reshape them. They do not cancel elections; they manage them. They do not censor information outright; they overwhelm it. And because each step appears legal, or at least defensible, resistance often arrives too late, too fragmented, or too exhausted to be effective.

This chapter is about pattern recognition. What happened at the Justice Department was not unique. Similar sequences have unfolded in Hungary, Poland, Turkey, Venezuela, and El Salvador. Different countries. Different leaders. The same structure. That is not coincidence.

Modern authoritarians learn from one another. They share tactics, adapt strategies, refine what works, and discard what does not. Over time, those methods have hardened into something recognizable—a playbook.

Understanding that playbook changes how everything looks. It makes it possible to see what is happening before institutions fail. It explains why resistance so often feels reactive and behind the curve. And it reveals where authoritarian movements are most vulnerable. Authoritarian power appears overwhelming only when its structure is invisible. Once the pattern is visible, inevitability collapses.

This chapter will walk through the core tactics modern authoritarians use—not in theory and not as isolated events, but as a coordinated strategy. We will examine how truth is undermined, how enemies are manufactured, how institutions are captured, how opposition is exhausted, and how extremes are normalized. Each tactic reinforces the others. Each depends on timing, attention, and fatigue.

The goal here is not alarm. It is precision. Resistance works best when it understands what it is interrupting.

In the next section, we begin with the foundation of the entire playbook—not repression or force, but the systematic destruction of shared reality. When people can no longer agree on what is true, everything else becomes possible.

Section 2

When Truth Stops Holding

Before authoritarians can take control of institutions, they have to do something more basic. They have to make truth unreliable. Not invisible. Not illegal. Just unstable. Democracy depends on a fragile assumption: that people can disagree about values while still agreeing about facts. When that assumption collapses, accountability collapses with it.

It is tempting to think authoritarianism begins with lies. But lying alone is not enough. Politicians have always lied. Propaganda has always existed. What distinguishes modern authoritarianism is not deception, but disorientation. The goal is not to convince people of a single false story. It is to make every story feel questionable. When that happens, truth no longer constrains power.

You can see this shift when contradiction stops being embarrassing. Leaders say one thing in the morning and the opposite in the afternoon. Evidence disproves a claim, and the claim is repeated anyway. Facts are dismissed not with counter-facts, but with ridicule. At first, this feels shocking. Then it feels exhausting. Eventually, it feels pointless to keep track. That is the moment authoritarianism depends on.

This strategy works because it exploits how human cognition actually functions. Most people cannot verify facts independently. Modern life is too complex for that. Instead, we rely on shortcuts to understand the world: trusted institutions, shared expertise, professional norms, and social consensus. Democracy functions because these shortcuts are usually reliable. Authoritarianism works by breaking trust in the shortcuts themselves.

The first move is flooding. Instead of suppressing information, authoritarians overwhelm it. Contradictory claims circulate at the same time. Rumors move faster than corrections. Outrage replaces explanation. The volume alone makes careful evaluation impossible. When people feel overloaded, they do not become better thinkers. They become selective. They retreat to familiar sources, accept explanations that align with identity, and disengage from complexity. Truth becomes optional.

The second move is attacking the institutions that validate reality. Journalists are labeled enemies. Scientists become elites. Judges are cast as partisans. Civil servants are reframed as hidden actors. The aim is not to prove these institutions wrong, but to make them suspect. Once trust erodes, evidence loses its force. A fact from a discredited source no longer functions as a fact. It becomes just another opinion.

The third move is weaponizing skepticism. Authoritarians do not reject critical thinking; they distort it. Every inconvenient fact is treated as biased. Every study is questioned. Every source is accused of hidden motives. But this skepticism is applied selectively. Claims that support power are accepted instantly. Claims that challenge it face impossible standards of proof. The result is a performance of rigor that ensures only one version of reality survives scrutiny.

Over time, something more dangerous happens. People stop asking whether something is true. They start asking whose side it is on. At that point, evidence no longer persuades. Identity does.

This is why fact-checking alone so often fails. Corrections arrive late. They demand attention and effort. They assume the audience still trusts the institutions issuing them. When those conditions no longer exist, more facts do not restore reality. They deepen fatigue.

The result is not ignorance, but exhaustion around truth itself. People still care. They still hold values. But they stop believing that understanding what is true will change anything. Disengagement follows, and disengagement creates the space authoritarian power needs to advance.

This collapse of shared reality is not a side effect. It is the foundation. Once truth stops holding, accountability weakens. Once accountability weakens, institutions become vulnerable. Once institutions erode, resistance becomes reactive and fragmented. That is why authoritarian movements invest so heavily here, long before moving openly against courts, elections, or civil service protections.

In the next section, we'll look at what happens once reality fractures—how fear is redirected, how enemies are manufactured, and why authoritarian movements always need someone inside the nation to blame. When truth dissolves, identity rushes in to take its place.

Section 3

How Enemies Are Made

Once shared reality breaks down, something else moves quickly to fill the gap: fear. When people are no longer sure what is true, they reach for something that feels solid. Fear offers that solidity when facts no longer do. Authoritarian movements understand this well. They do not simply exploit fear. They organize it.

Fear on its own is chaotic. People feel anxious, unsettled, and overwhelmed, but they do not know where to direct that energy. Left unshaped, fear can turn inward, producing paralysis or withdrawal. Authoritarian movements intervene at this point by giving fear direction. They tell people who to fear.

The process is deliberate. Complex problems are simplified. Economic instability is reframed as the fault of outsiders. Cultural change becomes a threat. Institutional failure is recast as sabotage. Ambiguity disappears. Instead of systems, there are villains. Instead of uncertainty, there is intention. Instead of structural causes, there are enemies. This is not about accuracy. It is about emotional efficiency.

Authoritarian movements consistently identify two categories of enemies. The first are internal enemies—people who live within the nation but are framed as outsiders nonetheless. Journalists, activists, minority groups, political opponents, civil servants, and intellectuals are all common targets. They are accused of disloyalty and corruption, of weakening the nation from within. Crucially, they are not portrayed as merely wrong. They are portrayed as dangerous.

The second category is external enemies. Foreign nations, immigrants, international institutions, and global elites serve this role. External enemies explain decline without requiring self-reflection. They allow leaders to present themselves as defenders rather than failures. If the nation is under attack, then the concentration of power can be justified as protection.

What matters most is not which group is targeted, but how fear is attached to identity. Once fear becomes personal, rational debate becomes nearly impossible. People are no longer weighing evidence. They are defending who they are.

This is why authoritarian rhetoric relies so heavily on language of invasion, contamination, and decay. The nation is said to be overrun. Values are described as erased. Culture is portrayed as being destroyed. These metaphors bypass reasoning and trigger instinct. They collapse complexity into urgency, and urgency crowds out deliberation.

Over time, this has a predictable effect on those in the middle—the enablers and the disengaged. People who might otherwise resist authoritarian behavior begin to tolerate it because it feels like a response to danger. *I don't like how far this is going, but something has to be done. This isn't ideal, but these are extraordinary times.* Fear lowers standards. Actions that once seemed unacceptable become understandable, then defensible, and eventually routine.

This is how authoritarian movements turn difference into threat. They do not need to invent hatred. They only need to concentrate anxiety. Once that happens, power can move quickly, because people are no longer asking whether actions are lawful or democratic. They are asking whether they feel protected.

There is one final consequence worth naming. As enemies are constantly emphasized, trust within society erodes. People become suspicious of one another. Coalitions fracture. Solidarity weakens. Resistance becomes harder to sustain, because the mutual trust required for collective action has been deliberately damaged. Authoritarianism does not only attack institutions. It attacks the social fabric that makes resistance possible.

In the next section, we'll examine how this fear-based division is reinforced through institutions themselves—how courts are reshaped, how civil service protections are removed, and how loyalty replaces competence. Once enemies are defined, the next step is to ensure that no one inside the system can effectively resist.

Section 4

Capturing Institutions Without Breaking Them

Authoritarians rarely need to destroy institutions. They only need to control them. Breaking institutions provokes resistance. Capturing them produces compliance. And capture almost always presents itself as lawful.

The first move is personnel. Positions that once prioritized competence are quietly redefined around loyalty. Career professionals are replaced, sidelined, or pressured to leave. Temporary appointments become permanent. Oversight roles are weakened or simply left unfilled. Nothing dramatic appears to happen, but expertise steadily drains from the system. Once that occurs, rules still exist, yet fewer people remain who know how—or feel empowered—to enforce them properly.

The second move is procedural. Rules are altered in ways that sound technical rather than ideological. Eligibility requirements shift. Decision timelines are shortened. Appeal processes are narrowed. Oversight thresholds are raised. Each change can be defended on its own. Taken together, they tilt the system. What once required justification now requires permission to challenge.

The third move is intimidation without overt repression. Formal protections remain in place, but informal consequences begin to appear. Careers stall. Budgets shrink. Investigations multiply. Transfers happen for "operational reasons." People learn quickly which decisions invite trouble and which bring quiet rewards. Authoritarian systems do not require universal compliance. They need only enough people to anticipate consequences in advance.

This is how independence disappears without being abolished. Judges remain judges. Civil servants remain civil servants. Regulators remain regulators. But discretion narrows. Choices become cautious. Enforcement grows selective.

Accountability becomes inconsistent. From the outside, institutions appear intact. From the inside, they are hollowed.

Alongside these structural changes comes a psychological shift. People inside institutions begin to tell themselves a familiar story: *If I stay, I can still do some good. If I leave, someone worse will take my place. This is temporary. I am protecting the system from within.* Sometimes that is true. Often, it is not. Over time, adaptation turns into normalization, and normalization turns into participation.

This is one reason authoritarian capture is so difficult to reverse. Once institutions adjust to new expectations, reversing course feels disruptive, even dangerous. Procedures have changed. Personnel have changed. Incentives have changed. What once felt like erosion begins to feel like stability.

The most important point is this: authoritarian systems rely less on coercion than on anticipation. People do not need to be told what to do. They learn what not to do. Once that lesson spreads, power no longer needs to intervene directly. The system begins to police itself.

This is why resistance that focuses only on elections or leadership personalities often misses the deeper danger. By the time authoritarian capture is visible at the top, it is usually embedded far below—in job descriptions, procedures, internal norms, and quiet expectations no one ever writes down.

In the next section, we'll look at how this institutional capture is reinforced over time—how exhaustion is manufactured, how constant crisis prevents reflection, and why authoritarian systems thrive when everything feels urgent. Once institutions are bent, the final task is to make resistance feel impossible to sustain.

Section 5

Exhaustion as a Strategy

Authoritarian systems rarely defeat resistance outright. They wear it down.

Exhaustion is not an accident. It is a strategy.

The pace never slows. Crises overlap. Scandals accumulate. Contradictions multiply. Just as attention settles on one issue, another erupts. Before outrage can harden into action, it is displaced by something new. Nothing ever fully resolves. Everything demands immediate response. This constant urgency keeps people reactive rather than reflective.

The effect is cumulative. Each incident on its own feels manageable. Together, they become overwhelming. People begin to lose track. What happened last week? Which rule changed? Which line was crossed? Confusion is not always deliberate, but it is always useful. When people cannot keep events straight, accountability weakens.

Exhaustion also fragments opposition. Different groups focus on different emergencies. Coalitions strain under constant pressure. Internal disagreements intensify. When energy is limited, people protect their own corner. Coordination gives way to triage, and triage rarely produces long-term strategy.

There is an emotional cost as well. Outrage burns hot, but briefly. Sustained anger is draining. Sustained vigilance even more so. Over time, people disengage— not because they stop caring, but because caring becomes too costly. *I can't keep up. I need a break. I'll tune back in later.* Later rarely arrives.

Authoritarian systems understand this cycle. They do not fear protest that burns out in days or outrage that spikes and fades. They fear organized persistence. So they shape the environment to make persistence feel unbearable.

Contradiction is one of the most effective tools. Statements change constantly. Positions reverse. Promises dissolve. Critics point out inconsistencies. Supporters shrug. The goal is not coherence. It is fatigue. If nothing stays true long enough to be contested, resistance never stabilizes.

Another tool is normalization through repetition. What shocks at first becomes familiar. Language hardens. Behavior escalates. Boundaries shift. People adjust, not because they approve, but because adjustment is easier than constant alarm. This is how extremes become routine.

Eventually, exhaustion changes how people evaluate risk. Early on, the questions are ethical and legal. *Is this right? Is this acceptable?* Later, the question becomes practical. *Is it worth the effort to fight this?* That shift is decisive. When resistance feels optional, power becomes durable.

This is the final phase of the playbook. Not repression. Not terror. Resignation. When enough people believe nothing can be done, authoritarian systems no longer need to push. They simply continue.

Exhaustion, however, is not inevitable. It is produced—and what is produced can be disrupted. In the next section, we'll look at the weakest point in the entire playbook: where authoritarian systems, despite their apparent strength, are most vulnerable. What wears people down also reveals where resistance can regain footing —if it is designed differently.

Section 6

Where the Playbook Breaks

Up to this point, the playbook can feel unsettlingly effective. Truth is destabilized. Fear is organized. Institutions are captured. Exhaustion sets in. From the outside, authoritarian systems begin to look unstoppable. That impression, however, is misleading. The same strategies that allow authoritarianism to advance also create its most serious weaknesses.

Authoritarian systems depend on continuous pressure. They require constant narrative control, constant crisis, and constant enforcement of loyalty. They cannot pause. The moment attention stabilizes, contradictions become visible. The moment fear subsides, legitimacy weakens. The moment exhaustion lifts, coordination becomes possible again. This is not a sign of strength. It is a structural vulnerability.

Authoritarian power also scales poorly. It centralizes decision-making while expanding responsibility, concentrating authority even as problems multiply. Over time, this creates bottlenecks. Too many decisions flow upward. Too many crises require personal intervention. Too many institutions wait for signals rather than acting independently. What once felt decisive begins to feel brittle.

There is a deeper contradiction at work. Authoritarian systems demand loyalty, but they cannot generate trust. Fear can enforce compliance, but it does not produce commitment. As a result, information degrades. People tell leaders what they think is safe to say. Problems are concealed until they become crises. Reality is filtered upward through caution and self-protection. This is why authoritarian systems often appear confident right up until they fail. They are poorly informed by design.

Another weakness lies in overreach. When resistance is framed as an existential threat, even small challenges feel intolerable. Criticism becomes dangerous. Dissent feels destabilizing. Independent action appears disloyal. Control tightens. Punishments increase. Rules proliferate. Each step provokes new resistance, which is then used to justify further escalation. The system becomes trapped in its own feedback loop.

Most importantly, authoritarian power depends less on belief than on passivity. It does not require mass support. It requires mass withdrawal. People do not have to agree. They only have to stop engaging. That means when engagement reappears—strategically, collectively, and persistently—the system begins to strain. Not immediately. Not dramatically. But measurably.

This is where many analyses stop short. They describe authoritarianism as overwhelming, but offer no path forward that does not rely on heroism or collapse. That is not realistic. What matters is not defeating authoritarian systems outright. It is interrupting their momentum—slowing consolidation, raising costs, and protecting institutions long enough for participation to matter again. This kind of resistance does not look like constant protest. It looks like design.

The playbook ultimately breaks where it assumes exhaustion is permanent. It is not. Exhaustion is a condition of environment. Change the environment, and behavior changes with it. People re-engage when action feels effective. They persist when effort compounds. They coordinate when roles are clear. Authoritarian systems cannot prevent this without abandoning the very constraints that allow them to function.

This chapter has traced how democratic erosion happens without drama. The next chapter turns toward how resistance can be built without burnout—not by matching authoritarian intensity, but by exploiting its limits; not by reacting faster, but by acting more deliberately; not by trying to awaken everyone, but by organizing the middle. The most effective resistance does not confront the playbook head-on. It steps around it.

CHAPTER 4
Breaking the Authoritarian Spell

Section 1

Why Authoritarianism Feels Right

To understand how authoritarian movements take hold, we need to begin with an uncomfortable truth. They do not succeed because people are stupid, cruel, or secretly longing for tyranny. They succeed because they meet real human needs—needs that modern life often leaves unmet.

Most people do not join authoritarian movements because of ideology. They join because something is missing. Belonging. Certainty. Purpose. Status. A sense that their actions matter. Authoritarian systems are effective because they promise to fill these gaps quickly and convincingly.

This is why arguments alone rarely work. If authoritarianism were simply about false beliefs, correcting the facts would be enough. But it is not. It is about how people feel in a world that often seems unstable, impersonal, and overwhelming.

Authoritarian movements offer something deceptively simple. They tell people that they belong, that they are seen, and that they are part of something important. They explain the chaos by giving it a cause and present a clear way forward. When life feels fragmented, this kind of clarity can feel like relief.

That appeal becomes stronger during periods of rapid change—economic uncertainty, cultural shifts, technological acceleration, and information overload. When the world feels unpredictable, many people do not ask for more freedom. They ask for order. They do not ask for complexity. They ask for certainty.

What matters here is something subtle. Most people drawn toward authoritarianism are not trying to dominate others. They are trying to regain stability. They want to feel anchored again. Authoritarian movements exploit this desire by reframing control as protection.

Strong leaders are presented not as tyrants, but as guardians. Rules are framed not as restrictions, but as safeguards. Conformity is described not as obedience, but as unity. In this way, authoritarianism does not feel like giving something up. It feels like getting something back.

This is why moral condemnation so often backfires. Calling people foolish, hateful, or dangerous does not weaken authoritarian appeal; it strengthens it. Authoritarian movements thrive on the belief that outsiders do not understand—or do not care. Every dismissal reinforces that story.

If we want to break the authoritarian spell, we have to understand its emotional logic. Not to excuse it. Not to normalize it. But to see clearly what it offers, and why it works.

This chapter is not about debating ideology. It is about understanding the human terrain on which ideology lands. Because if we do not address the needs authoritarianism exploits, we will keep fighting symptoms while leaving the cause intact.

In the next section, we'll look more closely at one of the most powerful of those needs: belonging—and how authoritarian movements turn isolation into loyalty.

Section 2

How Belonging Becomes Loyalty

Belonging is not a political preference. It is a human need. Long before people argue about ideology, they are asking a quieter question, often without realizing it: *Where do I fit?* When that question goes unanswered for too long, people do not become neutral. They become vulnerable.

Modern life produces isolation quietly. People move more often. Work is less stable. Community institutions weaken. Social roles blur. Even as communication increases, connection thins. Many people find themselves surrounded by others and alone at the same time. This is the terrain authoritarian movements exploit.

Authoritarian groups are very good at doing something basic: they gather people. Not only online, but emotionally. They offer shared language, shared symbols, shared enemies, and shared rituals. These things matter more than arguments ever could, because belonging does not begin with belief. It begins with recognition.

The invitation is usually subtle. *You're not crazy. You see what others refuse to admit. You've been ignored, but you matter. People like you built this country.* At first, this feels validating. Someone is finally naming the frustration. Someone is listening. And once people feel seen, loyalty begins to form.

What follows is gradual but consequential. Belonging slowly turns into obligation. Group identity becomes tied to moral worth. Dissent starts to feel like betrayal. Criticism feels like attack. People do not simply agree anymore; they defend. This is the moment when loyalty begins to replace deliberation.

Authoritarian movements reinforce this shift constantly. Us and them. Insiders and outsiders. The loyal and the disloyal. Boundaries tighten, not because leaders always demand it explicitly, but because belonging becomes conditional. Stay inside the group and you are protected. Step outside it and you are exposed. Fear does the rest.

What makes this dynamic so powerful is that it does not feel coercive. It feels relational. People are not obeying orders. They are protecting a connection, preserving an identity, and avoiding loss.

Once belonging is secured, facts lose influence. Evidence that threatens the group is discounted. Contradictions are reframed as attacks. Doubt is treated as weakness. Not because people stop thinking, but because thinking now happens inside a social boundary. Truth becomes whatever keeps the group intact.

This is why arguing harder so often fails. Facts that challenge belonging feel like attempts to exile someone from the group, and exile is terrifying. People double down not out of ignorance, but out of self-protection.

Breaking this dynamic requires care. When resistance attacks belonging directly, it strengthens authoritarian loyalty. When it mocks or shames, it confirms the narrative of exclusion. The critical question, then, is not *how do we defeat authoritarian belief*, but *how do we offer belonging without demanding loyalty*.

That shift changes everything. It moves resistance away from confrontation and toward reconstruction. It asks how democratic spaces can once again feel meaningful, participatory, and human—not abstract, distant, or dismissive, but lived.

In the next section, we'll examine how authoritarian movements turn belonging into moral certainty, and why that certainty feels so calming in a world full of ambiguity. Once belonging is secured, the next step is to simplify the world itself.

Section 3

Why Moral Certainty Feels Like Safety

Uncertainty is uncomfortable—not intellectually, but emotionally. Living with ambiguity requires patience, humility, and a willingness to trust that answers will emerge over time. During periods of instability, those qualities are difficult to sustain. Authoritarian movements offer a different bargain. They remove uncertainty.

Moral certainty simplifies the world. Good and bad are clearly defined. Right and wrong feel obvious. Questions fade. In a complex and shifting environment, that simplicity can feel like relief. People no longer have to weigh competing claims, tolerate doubt, or sit with discomfort. They can act.

This is not because people are incapable of complexity. It is because complexity is exhausting. When life feels unstable, moral clarity becomes a form of rest. It allows people to stop searching.

Authoritarian narratives are designed to deliver this rest. They divide the world into clean categories, assign blame decisively, and explain failure without ambiguity. If something goes wrong, there is a reason. If people suffer, someone is responsible. If progress stalls, someone is in the way. Nothing is accidental. Nothing is uncertain.

That certainty restores a sense of control. When people feel morally certain, they feel anchored and oriented. They feel capable of acting decisively, even if the action itself changes very little. Often, the feeling of decisiveness matters more than the outcome.

This helps explain why authoritarian movements escalate moral language. Critics are not mistaken; they are corrupt. Opponents are not wrong; they are dangerous. Differences are not tolerable; they are threats. Moral language intensifies because it stabilizes identity. Once someone believes they are on the side of good, doubt becomes unnecessary—and even suspect.

There is a cost to this clarity. Moral certainty narrows perception. It discourages listening, collapses nuance, and frames compromise as weakness. As compromise disappears, democracy struggles to function. Democratic systems depend on disagreement without dehumanization. Authoritarian systems replace that process with righteousness.

This is why authoritarian systems often feel emotionally calm on the inside, even as they generate chaos outside. Followers feel protected by certainty. Leaders feel justified by moral framing. Dissent becomes dangerous because it threatens the emotional structure holding everything together.

Breaking this pattern does not require attacking people's values. It requires reintroducing tolerable uncertainty—spaces where disagreement does not threaten belonging, conversations where doubt is allowed without punishment, and collective action that does not demand moral purity. This work is slow, but it is the only work that loosens the grip of false certainty.

Certainty offered too cheaply always comes at a price. It demands obedience. It demands exclusion. And eventually, it demands sacrifice—often from the very people who believed it would protect them.

In the next section, we'll look at the final emotional mechanism authoritarianism relies on. Not fear. Not belonging. Not certainty. But relief—how authoritarian systems turn resignation into stability, and why that relief is one of the hardest spells to break.

Section 4

The Comfort of Giving Up

After fear has been organized, belonging has hardened into loyalty, and moral certainty has simplified the world, something quieter takes hold. Relief.

Living in constant tension is exhausting. Staying alert, evaluating every claim, worrying about every outcome—over time, that level of vigilance becomes unsustainable. Eventually, people look for rest. Authoritarian systems offer it, not openly or explicitly, but effectively.

That relief comes from surrendering responsibility. From no longer having to decide what is true, question authority, or worry about outcomes beyond one's control. Someone else is in charge now. And for many people, that feels like a weight lifting.

This is where support for authoritarian systems is often misunderstood. It is assumed to reflect enthusiasm or deep conviction. In reality, it frequently reflects fatigue. People do not necessarily believe everything they are told. They simply stop resisting.

Resignation has a calming quality. When expectations are lowered, disappointment fades. When agency is relinquished, anxiety softens. When responsibility shifts upward, daily life feels simpler. *I can't change this. So I'll adapt. I'll focus on my own life.* These are not immoral thoughts. They are survival strategies.

Authoritarian systems benefit enormously from this shift. They do not require constant loyalty, active participation, or even belief. What they need is compliance without friction. Resignation provides exactly that.

Over time, resignation turns into stability. Not because conditions improve, but because struggle recedes. People stop expecting accountability. They stop imagining alternatives. They stop noticing erosion as erosion. The system settles.

This helps explain why authoritarian systems often feel strangely calm after periods of upheaval. Not peaceful, but quiet. Opposition retreats into private spaces. Public life narrows. Politics becomes background noise. For many people, that quiet feels preferable to constant conflict.

The cost, of course, is paid later. Resignation trades short-term relief for long-term vulnerability. Rights weaken quietly. Institutions hollow out. Abuses normalize. By the time consequences are felt directly, options are fewer. But when resignation first sets in, those costs feel distant—abstract.

Breaking this final spell is difficult because it asks people to give up comfort. Not excitement. Not certainty. Rest. It requires re-engaging with complexity and uncertainty, and that cannot be done through pressure or alarm. It has to be done by changing what engagement feels like.

This is why resistance fails when it relies only on warning. Fear competes poorly with relief. Urgency competes poorly with rest. If democratic participation feels like endless strain, people will choose withdrawal—even when they understand the risks.

Breaking the authoritarian spell, then, is not about waking people up. It is about making participation sustainable again—restoring agency without exhaustion, offering belonging without obedience, and creating certainty without rigidity. This is not primarily a messaging challenge. It is a design challenge.

This chapter has mapped the emotional terrain authoritarian systems exploit. The next chapter turns fully toward reconstruction—not grand gestures or heroic sacrifice, but ways resistance can be built so that people can actually live with it over time. Because the strongest opposition to authoritarianism is not outrage. It is endurance.

Section 5

What This Looks Like

Breaking the authoritarian spell does not require constant vigilance or heroic resistance. In practice, it looks quieter—and more ordinary—than most people expect. It begins with a change in posture rather than a surge of activity.

People stop treating politics as a permanent emergency that demands full attention, and stop treating disengagement as the only alternative. Instead, participation becomes bounded. It has edges. It fits around work, family, disagreement, and fatigue. People do not ask, How much can I give? They ask, What can I carry without burning out—and carry again next month?

Belonging, in this model, is rebuilt deliberately and modestly. Not through mass rallies or identity-driven loyalty, but through shared responsibility in small, durable settings. Neighborhood associations, professional organizations, local boards, unions, faith communities, volunteer groups, and civic institutions begin to matter again—not as symbols, but as places where people are known, disagreements are tolerated, and participation does not require moral purity.

In these spaces, belonging is not conditional on agreement. People are allowed to show up inconsistently, to disagree without being cast out, and to step back without being shamed. This matters more than persuasion. When people feel they can remain part of a community without surrendering judgment, authoritarian loyalty loses much of its emotional pull.

Moral certainty loosens not through argument, but through practice. People encounter complexity in lived form—working alongside others who disagree, negotiating tradeoffs, and seeing how decisions actually get made. Certainty gives way to familiarity. Disagreement becomes normal rather than threatening. Over time, the need for simplified enemies diminishes, not because beliefs change overnight, but because reality becomes harder to flatten.

Participation also changes shape. Instead of constant reaction to national crises, effort shifts toward maintenance. Someone watches a local school board agenda. Someone else attends a budget hearing twice a year. Someone supports an independent institution quietly and consistently. These acts rarely feel dramatic. They do not produce constant emotional reward. But they accumulate. They create friction where authoritarian systems expect passivity.

Crucially, no one is asked to do everything. Responsibility is distributed. Roles rotate. People take breaks and return. The system does not depend on a few exhausted individuals carrying the weight indefinitely. This is how endurance is built —not through intensity, but through repetition.

What is deliberately absent from this model is just as important. There is no demand for constant outrage. No requirement to track every development. No expectation that everyone must be equally informed or equally active at all times. The goal is not total awareness, but sufficient presence. Not constant resistance, but reliable resistance.

When participation is designed this way, resignation becomes less attractive. The quiet relief authoritarian systems offer—someone else will handle it—loses its appeal when people experience agency without exhaustion. Engagement no longer feels like strain layered on top of an already full life. It feels like part of life.

This is how the authoritarian spell weakens. Not through awakening, confrontation, or collapse—but through the slow reintroduction of shared responsibility that people can actually live with.

The next chapter moves from this emotional terrain into structure. It examines how democratic solidarity can be built intentionally—so that participation remains possible not just in moments of crisis, but over time.

CHAPTER 5
Creating Democratic Solidarity

Section 1

Solidarity Is Built, Not Declared

By now, a pattern should be clear. Authoritarian systems do not win because people stop caring. They win because caring becomes unsustainable. Resistance burns hot and then burns out. Outrage surges and collapses into fatigue. People show up—briefly—and then disappear. The problem is not motivation. It is design.

Most resistance movements treat solidarity as an emotion. Something people feel in moments of crisis. Something that appears when the stakes are high enough and can be summoned through urgency or moral appeal. That approach fails reliably. Emotions spike, but they do not endure.

Authoritarian systems understand this better than their opponents. They do not rely on passion. They rely on structure. Loyalty is embedded in routines. Rewards and punishments are distributed consistently. Participation becomes habitual rather than heroic. Democratic resistance often tries to compete at the level of feeling. It should not. It should compete at the level of infrastructure.

Solidarity that lasts is not declared. It is built. It emerges through systems that make participation visible, shared, effective, and sustainable. When people can see that their effort matters—and that it compounds over time—they stay. When effort feels isolated or purely symbolic, they leave.

This is the shift Chapter 5 introduces. It moves away from protest as performance, from solidarity as sentiment, and from resistance as constant emergency. In their place, it argues for something quieter and stronger: durable democratic solidarity.

Solidarity of this kind has several defining characteristics. It is practical. People do not need to agree on everything; they need to be able to do something together. It is distributed. Responsibility is shared, no one is indispensable, and no one burns out alone. And it is embedded. Participation fits into ordinary life rather than demanding constant sacrifice or moral purity. These characteristics are not aspirational. They are structural.

This is where many movements go wrong. They confuse scale with strength, visibility with power, and mobilization with durability. A movement can attract millions and still collapse if participation is exhausting or unclear. Authoritarian systems do not fear numbers. They fear organized persistence.

Creating democratic solidarity means designing for that persistence. It requires asking different questions. Not *how do we get people to show up*, but *how do we make participation easy to repeat*. Not *how do we raise awareness*, but *how do we connect awareness to action that actually constrains power*.

This chapter is not about slogans. It is about architecture—the kinds of structures that allow ordinary people to remain engaged without burning out, the kinds of roles that enable contribution without overexposure, and the kinds of networks that can survive disappointment, disagreement, and slow progress.

We will examine three foundations that make durable solidarity possible: economic foundations, because material security shapes participation; cultural foundations, because shared meaning sustains commitment; and political foundations, because power must be exercised, not just expressed. Each will be approached not as an ideal, but as a design problem with real constraints. No heroics required.

The goal here is modest, but consequential. Not to defeat authoritarianism in a single wave, but to interrupt its momentum—to slow consolidation, protect space for participation, and make withdrawal less attractive than engagement.

Solidarity built this way does not feel dramatic. It feels routine. Sometimes frustrating. Occasionally boring. And that is precisely why it works. Authoritarian systems thrive on intensity and exhaustion. Democratic systems survive on continuity.

In the next section, we'll begin with the most overlooked foundation of all: the economic conditions that make sustained participation possible—or impossible.

People cannot defend democracy if their lives are constantly on the edge of collapse.

Section 2

The Economic Foundations of Solidarity

Before people can participate consistently in democratic life, something very basic has to be true: their lives have to be stable enough to allow it. This is not an ideological claim. It is a practical one.

People cannot sustain engagement when they are constantly struggling to meet basic needs. When work schedules change unpredictably, healthcare is uncertain, housing is precarious, or a single emergency could trigger crisis, withdrawal is not apathy. It is self-preservation.

Authoritarian systems exploit this reality. They do not need to create economic insecurity; they only need to use it. When people are exhausted by instability, participation becomes a luxury. Attention narrows, tolerance for risk drops, and long-term thinking collapses into short-term coping. Democratic engagement—meetings, organizing, civic responsibility—starts to feel irresponsible, something reserved for people who have room in their lives.

This is why economic pressure is such a powerful political force. Not because it persuades people of a particular ideology, but because it shrinks the space in which choice can be exercised. When survival feels uncertain, flexibility disappears.

Durable solidarity requires the opposite condition. It requires room to breathe. Not comfort. Not prosperity. Breathing room—enough stability that people can show up again tomorrow, and enough predictability that participation does not feel like gambling with their future.

This is where many resistance movements falter. They assume commitment will override constraint, that people who care enough will find a way. Some will. Most will not—not because they lack concern, but because they cannot afford the cost.

Authoritarian movements understand this intuitively. They offer selective stability: jobs for the loyal, protection for supporters, relief for those who comply. This is not generosity. It is strategy. And it works because material security is tied directly to obedience.

Democratic solidarity cannot mirror that approach. It cannot promise protection in exchange for loyalty. But it *can* design participation that does not punish people for having limited capacity. That means roles that scale with availability, contributions that do not require constant presence, and structures that absorb absence without collapsing. Solidarity that lasts assumes uneven participation and plans for it.

Economic foundations also shape who participates. When engagement requires unpaid time, flexible schedules, or financial cushion, participation skews toward those who already have resources. Over time, this distorts the picture of "the public." Voices narrow, priorities shift, and legitimacy erodes. Those most affected by instability are the least able to shape responses to it—and that gap is corrosive.

Building democratic solidarity means accounting for this reality from the start. Not through moral appeal or urging sacrifice, but by designing systems that lower the cost of participation. When engagement fits into real lives, it becomes repeatable. When it demands constant strain, it disappears.

This is why economic foundations come first. Not because they solve everything, but because without them, everything else fails. Belonging fractures under stress. Culture becomes brittle. Political effort turns episodic.

Economic stability does not create democracy. But democracy cannot survive without it. And solidarity that ignores this reality becomes symbolic—visible, sincere, and unsustainable.

In the next section, we'll turn to the second foundation: culture. Not culture as ideology, but culture as shared meaning, shared norms, and shared expectations about how participation works. Even with stability, people disengage when participation feels empty, performative, or disconnected from everyday life.

Section 3

The Cultural Foundations of Solidarity

Even when people have enough stability to participate, another question remains: does participation actually mean anything? If engagement feels empty, performative, or disconnected from everyday life, people drift away—quietly and often permanently. This is not a failure of values. It is a failure of culture.

Culture, in this sense, is not ideology. It is not what people claim to believe. It is what participation feels like when it happens—who is welcomed, how disagreement is handled, what counts as contribution, and whether effort is recognized or ignored. These signals shape whether people stay.

Authoritarian movements are deliberate about cultural cues. They reward conformity, punish ambiguity, and offer simple narratives with clear status markers. Participation feels legible. People know where they stand. Democratic spaces often produce the opposite effect, usually without intending to.

In many democratic movements, participation comes with invisible rules. The right language. The right references. The right tone. The right priorities. These rules are rarely stated, but they are enforced socially. People learn them the hard way.

When participation feels like a test, people disengage. Not because they reject democracy, but because they do not want to be corrected, shamed, or sorted in public —especially when their lives already carry enough strain.

Durable solidarity requires a different cultural posture. One that treats disagreement as normal, allows partial participation, and values contribution over performance. Culture has to make imperfect engagement acceptable, because perfect engagement is unsustainable.

This does not mean abandoning standards. It means being clear about which standards actually matter: respect, good faith, and shared purpose. Not fluency. Not purity. Not constant alignment.

Continuity is another cultural signal that matters. People stay engaged when they can see a future for themselves in the work. Not a dramatic climax, but a place—a role they can grow into, a rhythm they can maintain, and a sense that showing up again matters more than showing up once.

Authoritarian cultures promise belonging through loyalty. Democratic cultures have to offer belonging through participation. That participation must feel real. It has to shape decisions, affect outcomes, and leave room for people to be human.

When culture fails, people rarely protest it. They simply leave. They stop attending, stop contributing, and stop identifying with the work. Once that happens, rebuilding trust becomes difficult.

This is why culture cannot be treated as decoration. It is infrastructure. It determines who remains engaged when progress slows, who stays when disagreements arise, and who returns after disappointment.

Economic stability makes participation possible. Culture makes it worthwhile. Without both, solidarity remains fragile—present in moments of crisis, absent when endurance is required.

In the next section, we'll turn to the final foundation: political infrastructure. Not elections alone, but the systems that translate participation into constraint. Solidarity that cannot act is eventually absorbed. Solidarity that can act does not need constant intensity to endure.

Section 4

The Political Foundations of Solidarity

Economic stability makes participation possible. Culture makes it meaningful.

But neither is enough on its own. For solidarity to endure, participation has to do something. It has to change outcomes, impose limits, and matter in ways people can see. That requires political infrastructure.

Political infrastructure is not the same as elections. Elections are moments. Infrastructure is continuity. It is the set of systems that connect participation to consequence over time, not just during peaks of attention. Without that connection, solidarity becomes expressive rather than effective. People show up, speak, and signal values—and then nothing happens.

This is where many democratic movements falter. They mobilize people brilliantly, generate attention, and articulate moral urgency, but lack pathways for turning that energy into durable constraint. *Who follows up? Who tracks decisions? Who applies pressure when attention fades? Who stays when headlines move on?* When those answers are unclear, power waits—and then proceeds.

Authoritarian systems are built around political infrastructure. They do not rely on constant enthusiasm. They rely on routine enforcement: appointments, procedures, internal discipline, and predictable consequences. That is why they are difficult to dislodge. They are not sustained by belief alone. They are sustained by systems.

Democratic solidarity has to be built in a similar way, without copying authoritarian control. That means designing participation so it can be repeated easily, responsibility is shared, disagreement can be survived, and engagement persists during quiet periods. When infrastructure is doing its job, this work happens largely out of sight. People do not feel heroic. They feel effective.

Political infrastructure also protects against burnout. When roles are clear, effort compounds. When responsibility is distributed, absence does not collapse the whole. When action is routinized, participation stops feeling like emergency labor. These conditions are what allow ordinary people to remain engaged over years rather than weeks.

Another essential function of political infrastructure is memory. Movements without infrastructure forget. They repeat mistakes, relearn lessons, and lose institutional knowledge as people cycle out. Infrastructure preserves learning. It carries experience forward even as participants change, allowing progress to accumulate rather than reset.

Without political infrastructure, solidarity remains vulnerable—prone to exhaustion, distraction, and easy neutralization. With it, solidarity becomes resilient. Not louder. Not purer. More durable.

This completes the framework. Economic foundations make participation possible. Cultural foundations make it meaningful. Political foundations make it effective. Remove any one, and solidarity collapses under pressure.

The rest of this book builds on these foundations—not through grand plans or idealized blueprints, but through practical ways to reduce burnout, distribute responsibility, protect participation, and interrupt authoritarian momentum. Democratic defense does not require everyone. It requires enough people, supported well enough, for long enough.

Section 5

What This Looks Like

When democratic solidarity is built rather than declared, it does not feel like a movement surging forward. It feels like systems quietly holding.

In practice, this means participation is organized around continuity, not intensity. People are not asked to show up constantly or to perform commitment publicly. Instead, they occupy roles that are limited, repeatable, and survivable. Someone attends a meeting once a month. Someone else tracks a narrow issue over time. Someone steps in for a season and steps back without apology. No single role carries moral weight. What matters is that the system continues.

Economic realities are treated as constraints, not character flaws. Participation assumes uneven capacity from the beginning. Some people can give time. Others can give attention, skills, or occasional presence. The structure absorbs these differences instead of punishing them. When someone disappears for a while, the work does not collapse—and when they return, they are not treated as suspect. This is how solidarity survives real life.

Culturally, solidarity looks unremarkable. Disagreement is expected. Awkward conversations happen. People are not sorted instantly into allies and enemies. Fluency is not a prerequisite. Participation is not a test. Over time, norms emerge that reward reliability more than rhetoric and presence more than performance. The atmosphere is not inspirational. It is functional—and that is its strength.

In these environments, belonging is not enforced through loyalty. It is sustained through usefulness. People stay because their contribution matters in visible ways, not because they are constantly affirmed. When someone shows up, does their part, and leaves knowing the work continues, trust accumulates quietly.

Politically, solidarity expresses itself through follow-through rather than spectacle. Attention does not spike and vanish. Someone remembers what was decided last time. Someone notices when a commitment is not honored. Someone asks the same question again six months later. Pressure is applied not loudly, but consistently. Power responds not to outrage, but to persistence.

Much of this work happens below the level of public recognition. There are no viral moments. No cathartic releases. Often, there is boredom. But boredom is not failure. It is a sign that participation has moved out of crisis mode and into maintenance mode—where endurance becomes possible.

What is absent here is as important as what is present. There is no demand for total alignment. No expectation of constant awareness. No belief that everyone must be activated at once. Solidarity does not depend on keeping people emotionally charged. It depends on keeping systems intact.

When solidarity is built this way, authoritarian momentum slows—not because it is confronted head-on, but because it loses the conditions it depends on. Withdrawal becomes less attractive. Resignation feels premature. Participation no longer feels like a sacrifice layered on top of an already strained life. It feels like a role that can be carried, set down, and carried again. This is democratic solidarity in practice. Not dramatic. Not pure. Durable.

CHAPTER 6
Winning Hearts and Minds

Section 1

Why Narrative Comes First

By the time most political arguments begin, the outcome is already constrained. Not by facts or evidence, but by meaning—by what people think is reasonable, what they think is possible, and what they believe people like them are allowed to want. This is the terrain where hearts and minds are shaped.

Most democratic movements treat persuasion as something that happens after positions are formed. First we decide what we believe. Then we explain it. Then we defend it. Authoritarian movements work in the opposite direction. They focus on shaping the environment in which belief forms long before explicit arguments appear.

This distinction matters because people rarely begin political thinking by weighing policy details. They start with quieter, more personal questions: *Who is this for? Where do I belong? What kind of person agrees with this? What does supporting this say about me?* Narrative answers these questions well before arguments ever enter the conversation.

This is why movements often lose debates they technically "win." They present strong evidence, make careful arguments, and cite credible sources—and still fail to persuade. The problem is not the quality of the argument. It is the timing. By the time the argument arrives, the frame is already set.

Winning hearts and minds is not about clever slogans or emotional manipulation. It is about shaping the context in which ideas are evaluated—what feels normal, what feels extreme, what feels moral, and what feels dangerous. Once those boundaries are established, facts are interpreted inside them rather than reshaping them.

This is why narrative work is not secondary to political strategy. It is foundational. Policy follows narrative. Coalitions follow narrative. Even outrage follows narrative. Before people argue about solutions, they have already—often unconsciously—agreed on what kind of world they believe they are living in.

Authoritarian movements understand this instinctively. They do not begin by listing policies. They begin by telling stories—stories about decline and betrayal, stories about enemies and restoration, stories about who belongs and who does not. These stories do not need to be accurate. They need to be coherent.

Democratic movements often resist this work. Narrative can feel manipulative, superficial, or less serious than policy. That hesitation is costly. Refusing to shape narrative does not create neutrality; it leaves the terrain open for others to define.

Narrative work does not replace truth. It determines whether truth can be heard. It does not eliminate complexity. It determines whether complexity feels threatening or navigable. It does not guarantee agreement. It determines whether disagreement remains possible without collapse.

This chapter is about reclaiming that work—not by copying authoritarian techniques or simplifying reality beyond recognition, but by understanding how meaning forms and learning to engage that process deliberately.

In the sections that follow, we'll look at how movements take control of narrative terrain, how stories create emotional connection without manipulation, how framing operates before debates begin, and how message discipline allows meaning to persist. None of this is about spin. It is about creating the conditions under which democratic ideas can survive.

Because democracy does not fail only when people stop voting. It fails when people stop imagining themselves inside it.

Section 2

Taking Control of the Narrative

Narratives rarely win by persuasion alone. More often, they win by being first. The first story people hear becomes the reference point for everything that follows. Later arguments are judged in relation to it—accepted, rejected, or ignored based on how well they fit within the initial frame. This is why controlling the narrative is not about dominating conversation. It is about setting the starting point.

Authoritarian movements grasp this instinctively. They do not wait to respond. They move first. They define the problem before anyone else has time to explain it differently, naming causes, assigning blame, and suggesting solutions in a single sweep. By the time critics speak, they are already arguing inside someone else's story.

This is why reactive messaging fails so often. When democratic movements spend their energy correcting false claims, they often reinforce the very narrative they are trying to dismantle. The frame remains intact. Only the details are contested.

Taking control of the narrative means refusing that trap. It shifts attention away from rebuttal and toward a different organizing idea—one that makes sense on its own terms. Not louder responses. Not faster fact-checks. A different lens altogether.

This does not require deception. It requires clarity. Narratives work when they explain why something matters before explaining what should be done. They answer questions people are already asking, even if they have not yet put those questions into words. *What's happening to us? Why does this feel harder than it should? Who benefits from the way things are now? What would "better" actually look like?* When a narrative answers those questions simply and consistently, it holds.

Consistency matters more than cleverness. Authoritarian narratives repeat the same core story across speeches, policies, media appearances, and symbolic acts. The details change, but the story does not. Over time, repetition produces familiarity, and familiarity begins to feel like legitimacy.

Democratic movements often move in the opposite direction. They adapt language constantly, tailor messaging to every audience, and chase nuance. Nuance has its place, but without a stable narrative core, meaning fragments. People hear pieces of the story without ever encountering the whole.

Taking control of the narrative does not mean flattening complexity. It means deciding which complexity comes first. It means choosing which ideas deserve repetition and which can wait. And it means protecting the narrative from dilution, even when dilution comes from well-intentioned allies.

This kind of work is demanding. It requires discipline and patience, and it often means accepting that not every argument will be answered immediately. But it is essential. Narratives do not only persuade opponents; they orient supporters. They signal what kind of participation is expected, what success looks like, and how long the work is likely to take.

Without narrative control, movements become reactive. They chase headlines, respond to provocations, and expend energy without building coherence. With narrative control, movements slow the tempo. They decide what matters, set expectations, and make persistence possible.

In the next section, we'll look at how narratives connect to emotion without manipulation—how stories can create identification rather than outrage, and how democratic movements can speak to lived experience without simplifying it beyond recognition. Winning hearts and minds is not about triggering feeling. It is about making meaning stable enough to live with.

Section 3

Speaking to Experience Without Exploitation

People are persuaded less by arguments than by recognition. Not recognition of their opinions, but recognition of their experience. When people feel that a movement understands what their lives are actually like, they listen. When they feel misunderstood or talked past, they disengage—no matter how strong the evidence may be.

Authoritarian movements exploit this instinct relentlessly. They do not begin by debating policy. They begin by naming frustration. They describe daily pressures in simple, emotionally charged language, often capturing resentment, loss, and confusion with unsettling accuracy. Only after that recognition do they redirect those feelings toward blame. This works because it starts with truth about experience, even when it ends in false explanation.

Democratic movements often skip this step. They move quickly to solutions, emphasize values, and present data. In doing so, they can unintentionally signal distance. Instead of hearing *"We understand,"* people hear *"We've already decided."* That gap matters more than most movements realize.

Speaking to experience does not mean validating every interpretation of that experience. It means beginning where people actually are. *What feels harder than it used to? What feels unfair? What feels confusing or out of reach?* When these questions are named openly, people feel seen—even if they do not yet agree with the conclusions that follow.

The danger arises when experience is exploited rather than acknowledged. Authoritarian narratives take real frustration and attach it to simple villains. They convert complexity into anger and transform uncertainty into certainty. The result is emotionally powerful but corrosive. Pain becomes fuel rather than something to be understood.

Democratic movements face a more difficult task. They must honor experience without weaponizing it. That means resisting exaggeration, avoiding simplification that distorts reality, and refusing the shortcut of turning frustration into rage. These choices can feel unsatisfying in the short term, but they protect credibility over time.

Instead, democratic narratives can do something quieter and more durable. They can normalize struggle without isolating people. They can name hardship without assigning enemies. They can connect individual experience to shared conditions rather than personal failure. This kind of storytelling does not spike emotion. It builds trust.

Trust grows when people hear their own lives reflected accurately—without flattery and without dismissal. When language feels grounded, tone feels respectful, and complexity is acknowledged rather than avoided. People do not need to be inflamed to care. They need to feel included.

This approach requires patience. It rarely produces viral moments or instant loyalty. But it creates something more durable. People remain engaged when they do not feel manipulated. They stay open when they do not feel judged. And they listen longer when they are not rushed toward conclusions.

Speaking to experience without exploitation also protects movements from backlash. Narratives that avoid demonization are harder to turn against themselves. Narratives that resist moral absolutism leave room for growth, learning, and disagreement. Over time, this keeps coalitions intact.

Winning hearts and minds, in this sense, is not about emotional dominance. It is about emotional accuracy—getting the texture of people's lives right, naming pressures honestly, and offering meaning without distortion.

In the next section, we'll look at how this kind of narrative discipline is sustained over time: how movements keep their story coherent across platforms, leaders, and moments of crisis. Meaning that fractures under pressure cannot support democratic work for long.

Section 4

Maintaining Narrative Discipline

Narratives rarely fail because they are wrong. More often, they fail because they fragment. Different voices emphasize different priorities. Messages shift with every new event. Urgency overrides coherence. Over time, people stop knowing what a movement actually stands for—and when meaning becomes unclear, commitment weakens.

Authoritarian movements avoid this problem by enforcing discipline. Their story stays simple. Its boundaries remain firm. Deviation is punished. Democratic movements cannot—and should not—operate this way. But they still need narrative discipline, not through control, but through clarity.

That discipline begins with a stable core: a small set of ideas repeated consistently even as circumstances change. Not slogans. Not talking points. Organizing truths—the kind that explain why the work exists and what problem it is actually trying to solve. When that core is clear, flexibility becomes possible without dilution.

Without a narrative core, movements become reactive. Every new crisis reshapes the message. Every internal disagreement becomes public confusion. Every spokesperson sounds as though they are speaking for a different cause. People outside the movement struggle to orient themselves, and when orientation is lost, engagement fades.

Maintaining narrative discipline does not mean saying the same thing everywhere. It means saying different things that point in the same direction. Stories adapt. Examples change. Language shifts by audience. But the underlying meaning remains stable. That stability is what allows people to recognize the movement even as contexts change.

Restraint is another essential element of discipline. Not every argument needs to be answered. Not every provocation deserves a response. Not every internal debate should unfold in public. Choosing silence is not weakness; it is often a way of protecting coherence.

Narrative discipline also depends on trust. When participants understand the core story, they do not need constant instruction. They can speak authentically without drifting into contradiction. This kind of shared understanding cannot be imposed through messaging. It develops gradually, through repetition and use.

One of the greatest threats to narrative discipline is speed. Social media rewards immediacy. News cycles reward reaction. Outrage rewards amplification. Democratic movements are often pulled into responding faster than they can think. Authoritarian movements exploit this dynamic, provoking responses precisely because reaction produces noise and fragmentation. Slowing down, in this context, becomes a form of resistance.

Narrative discipline allows movements to control tempo. It gives them the ability to choose when to speak, decide what matters, and preserve meaning even under pressure. Over time, that steadiness builds credibility. People trust movements that sound like they know who they are.

Winning hearts and minds is not about constant persuasion. It is about creating a stable field of meaning that people can step into and remain inside. That stability does more than convince. It anchors.

In the final section of this chapter, we'll look at how narratives translate into invitation—how movements welcome people in without demanding immediate agreement or total commitment. Hearts and minds do not change all at once. They change through entry points that feel safe enough to cross.

Section 5

Creating Entry Points, Not Tests

If narratives shape meaning, they also shape access. They determine who feels invited in and who feels quietly excluded. Many democratic movements make participation contingent on agreement. The right language. The right stance. The right level of certainty. Before people are welcomed, they are evaluated. That approach limits growth.

Authoritarian movements often behave very differently at the point of entry. They do not require full understanding or total commitment. They offer simple ways in—attend an event, share a symbol, repeat a phrase, join a group. Belief deepens later. Belonging comes first.

Democratic movements frequently reverse this order. They expect people to understand before they participate, to agree before they belong, and to commit before they explore. For many people, that sequence feels risky. So they remain outside.

Creating entry points means lowering the cost of initial participation—not by lowering standards, but by sequencing them. People need space to listen, observe, and try things out before being asked to take a stand. Entry points allow curiosity without exposure, participation without identity risk, and contribution without full alignment.

This matters most for people in the middle: those who feel uneasy, uncertain, or disengaged, but not hostile. They are rarely reached through confrontation. They respond more readily to invitation.

Entry points also protect movements from brittleness. When participation has only one acceptable form, disagreement quickly becomes exit. When there are multiple ways to engage, people can move within the space rather than leave it altogether. That flexibility strengthens movements over time.

Designing entry points requires intention. Clear roles that do not demand constant presence. Opportunities to contribute without public performance. Paths that allow people to deepen involvement gradually. Together, these structures communicate something simple and powerful: you do not have to be perfect to belong, you do not have to know everything to begin, and you do not have to commit forever to take a first step.

This is not about appealing to everyone. It is about avoiding unnecessary barriers. Barriers shrink coalitions. Entry points expand them. Over time, that difference compounds.

Winning hearts and minds is not about winning arguments. It is about widening participation—helping people imagine themselves inside democratic work, not as heroes or experts, but as contributors. That imagination often comes before belief.

This chapter has traced how meaning is shaped: how narratives set the field, how experience is acknowledged, how coherence is maintained, and how invitations replace tests. Together, these elements show how democratic movements can compete in the realm of meaning without manipulation, without exhaustion, and without abandoning truth.

In the next chapter, the focus shifts from persuasion to practice—how these narrative principles translate into concrete forms of engagement, what participation looks like when it is designed to endure, and how democratic work becomes something people can actually stay with.

Section 6

What This Looks Like

When winning hearts and minds is approached as narrative design rather than persuasion, it rarely feels like convincing anyone of anything.

In practice, it looks like movements speaking less often, but more consistently.

Fewer messages, repeated calmly over time. Language that does not chase every development or respond to every provocation. People hear the same core ideas across settings—not as slogans, but as orientation. Over time, familiarity replaces novelty, and meaning becomes easier to hold.

Narrative work of this kind often happens before anyone realizes it is happening. A conversation does not begin with an argument, but with recognition: Yes, this has been harder than it should be. No, you're not imagining it. Other people are struggling with this too. When people feel their experience has been named accurately, they remain open. When they feel rushed toward conclusions, they retreat.

Speaking this way requires restraint. Not every frustration is amplified. Not every injustice is framed as an emergency. Movements choose language that people can live with over language that produces immediate reaction. This often means accepting slower uptake and quieter responses in exchange for longer engagement.

Narrative discipline shows up most clearly in what movements decline to do. They do not argue inside hostile frames. They do not repeat opponents' language, even to reject it. They do not allow every internal disagreement to become a public referendum on identity. Silence is used deliberately—not to avoid conflict, but to protect coherence.

Entry points, when designed well, feel ordinary. Someone is invited to observe rather than speak. Someone is asked to help with a narrow task rather than declare a position. Someone is welcomed without being evaluated. Participation begins without exposure, and belief is allowed to follow rather than precede involvement.

This approach reshapes who stays. People who would never describe themselves as activists remain present because they are not asked to perform conviction. They are not required to master language, defend positions constantly, or signal moral alignment at every turn. They participate because the space feels navigable, not because they have been persuaded in full.

Over time, meaning stabilizes. People begin to recognize the movement not by its arguments, but by its tone—measured, grounded, resistant to panic. That steadiness becomes a form of credibility. When crises arise, the narrative does not need to change dramatically. It holds.

Winning hearts and minds in this way does not produce dramatic conversions. It produces fewer exits. Fewer people drift away quietly. Fewer decide the work is not for them. That absence of loss is easy to overlook, but it is decisive.

This is what narrative success looks like in democratic work. Not emotional dominance. Not viral persuasion. A field of meaning that people can step into without surrendering judgment—and remain inside without exhaustion.

The next chapter turns from narrative to participation itself: how these conditions of meaning connect to concrete roles, repeatable actions, and forms of engagement that allow democratic work to persist over time.

CHAPTER 7
The Economic Battlefield

Section 1

Power Leaves Footprints

When democratic movements confront authoritarian power, they often focus on what is most visible: speeches, elections, media narratives, public institutions. Those matter. But they are not where power begins.

Power leaves footprints. It shows up in money flows, supply chains, insurance policies, contracts, credit arrangements, and ownership structures. Authoritarian movements do not operate in abstraction. They depend on specific economic systems that make their power possible—and those systems can be examined, mapped, and pressured.

That is the shift this chapter introduces. Rather than directing resistance primarily at symbols or posture, it turns attention toward economic targeting: identifying the material structures that sustain authoritarian power and applying pressure where it actually has effect.

One of the most important lessons democratic movements have learned over the past several decades is that authoritarian power is rarely self-sustaining. It is financed, insured, serviced, and normalized through economic relationships that are often hidden in plain sight.

When movements fail, it is often because power is treated as monolithic—too large to touch, too entrenched to disrupt. When movements succeed, they usually do something different. They identify who enables the system, isolate which relationships matter most, and concentrate pressure precisely where leverage exists.

This is not abstract theory. Versions of this approach have appeared repeatedly across labor movements, civil-rights campaigns, environmental justice efforts, and anti-corruption struggles. When movements stop asking *who is in charge* and start asking *who makes this possible*, their strategic options expand.

Economic targeting changes the terrain. Instead of trying to persuade entire populations, movements apply pressure to a relatively small number of critical actors. Instead of appealing only to conscience, they introduce cost. Instead of shouting into systems designed to ignore protest, they engage mechanisms that cannot function without stability and trust.

This does not require matching authoritarian resources. It requires precision. Economic power depends on coordination. Coordination creates dependency. Dependency creates vulnerability. That vulnerability is the economic battlefield—and it exists even when political institutions are captured, courts are compromised, or elections are constrained. When formal democratic channels narrow or close, economic pressure often remains available.

This chapter is about learning to see that battlefield clearly. It explores how movements follow the money, map corporate and financial networks, and identify pressure points rather than symbolic targets—and how economic strategies can complement, rather than replace, narrative and political work.

Authoritarian systems do not collapse all at once. They weaken when the structures that support them begin to fracture—quietly, incrementally, and sometimes in ways that are only visible in retrospect.

In the next section, we'll look at the first step in that process: following the money. Not metaphorically, but concretely. Because understanding who funds power is often the beginning of learning how to limit it.

Section 2

Following the Money

Economic power rarely announces itself. It doesn't issue statements, give speeches, or explain its values. It moves quietly, through transactions.

If you want to understand who enables an authoritarian system, the most reliable place to look is not rhetoric. It's revenue.

Following the money means asking a different kind of question. Not *who supports this publicly*, but *who benefits materially if it continues*. Not *who claims neutrality*, but *who is exposed to loss if the system changes*. Questions like these cut through ideology quickly, because they point toward consequences rather than belief.

Most authoritarian systems rely on a surprisingly small set of economic relationships. Large investors. Key lenders. Insurance providers. Major suppliers. Critical service firms. These actors may not agree with authoritarian politics, and many would reject the label outright. But they make the system possible all the same.

This is the shift many movements miss. Faced with enabling institutions, they often try moral persuasion first. They appeal to values, call for responsibility, and issue public statements. Sometimes that works. Often it doesn't—because large economic actors respond most consistently not to persuasion, but to risk.

Following the money allows movements to introduce that risk deliberately. When a company's reputation becomes unstable, when regulatory scrutiny increases, when consumer trust erodes, or when investors begin asking uncomfortable questions, behavior changes. Not because hearts have been transformed, but because incentives have.

This does not mean attacking every company involved. That is a common mistake. Effective economic strategies are selective. They focus on relationships that are essential, actors that are sensitive to pressure, and disruptions that cascade through the system. Precision matters far more than volume.

Another misconception is that following the money requires technical expertise. It doesn't. Much of this information is public: corporate disclosures, financial reports, ownership records, contract announcements. The challenge is rarely access. It's focus.

Authoritarian systems benefit when power feels opaque—when money flows are complex, responsibility is diffuse, and no single actor appears accountable. Following the money restores visibility. It shows how abstract power is made concrete. And once power becomes concrete, it becomes contestable.

There is also a psychological shift that matters. Economic pressure changes the conversation. Instead of endless debates about belief, legitimacy, or intent, the question becomes practical: *Is this worth the cost?* That question doesn't require consensus. It only requires leverage.

Importantly, following the money does not replace other forms of resistance. It complements them. Narrative work creates legitimacy for pressure. Political organizing creates coordination. Economic strategies introduce constraint. Together, they alter the balance of power in ways that symbolic action alone cannot.

In the next section, we'll look at what happens after money is mapped—how movements decide where to apply pressure, and where not to. Following the money is only the first step. Choosing targets is where strategy truly begins.

Section 3

Choosing Pressure Points

Once money flows become visible, a new problem appears. There are suddenly too many places to intervene.

Every authoritarian system is supported by dozens—sometimes hundreds—of economic relationships. If movements attempt to pressure all of them at once, they spread themselves thin, exhaust their capacity, and often fail to change outcomes. This is where strategy begins to matter, and where restraint becomes a strength rather than a limitation.

Choosing pressure points means identifying where effort produces disproportionate effect. Not the loudest targets. Not the most symbolic ones. But the actors and relationships that are genuinely sensitive to disruption. That requires asking a different set of questions—questions oriented toward vulnerability rather than visibility.

> *Which actors are most exposed to reputational risk?*
> *Which rely on public trust to function?*
> *Which face regulatory scrutiny they would rather avoid?*
> *Which cannot easily replace a damaged relationship?*

Pressure works where vulnerability exists.

One of the most common mistakes movements make is confusing visibility with leverage. Highly visible corporations often appear powerful, but they are usually resilient. They absorb criticism, weather protests, and wait for attention to fade. Less visible actors—insurers, financiers, service providers, and intermediaries—are often more exposed. They operate on narrow margins of trust, depend on stability, and actively avoid controversy. In many cases, these quieter actors make more effective pressure points.

Another frequent error is overestimating the power of moral appeal. Public shaming can feel satisfying. It can generate attention and energize supporters. But without sustained follow-through, it rarely changes behavior. Pressure points work not because costs are dramatic, but because they accumulate. The most effective pressure is often persistent rather than spectacular.

For that reason, successful movements choose targets they can stay focused on. Targets that cannot easily deflect responsibility, that are connected to decision-makers, and that experience escalating consequences over time. Sustained attention is what allows pressure to matter.

Choosing pressure points also means deciding where not to act. Not every injustice can be addressed immediately. Not every enabling relationship can be disrupted at once. Selective engagement protects energy. It allows movements to learn, adapt, and build capacity instead of scattering effort across too many fronts.

There is a deeper strategic benefit to this focus. Concentrated pressure clarifies responsibility. When a small number of actors are identified repeatedly, narratives sharpen. Instead of diffuse outrage, people understand who is being asked to change, why that actor matters, and what outcome is being sought. That clarity strengthens participation.

Pressure points are also easier to coordinate around. Different groups can contribute in different ways—through research, communication, consumer action, or regulatory pressure—without duplicating effort. This is how economic strategies scale without requiring centralized control.

Importantly, choosing pressure points does not mean abandoning principle. It means sequencing action. Movements can care about many things at once. They cannot act on all of them simultaneously. Strategy is what allows values to translate into results.

In the next section, we'll look at how pressure is applied over time—not as a single confrontation, but as a campaign. Economic leverage rarely works in moments. It works through persistence.

Section 4

Sustaining Economic Pressure

Economic pressure rarely works all at once. It works over time. Many movements fail at this stage—not because their analysis is wrong, but because they expect a single action to produce immediate change. Economic power does not respond to moments. It responds to patterns.

Sustained pressure alters how risk is calculated. A single protest can be dismissed. A single boycott can be absorbed. A single news cycle can be waited out. But repeated disruption creates uncertainty, and uncertainty carries cost. Over time, it forces actors to reassess whether maintaining the status quo is still worth it.

This is why authoritarian systems try to exhaust economic campaigns quickly.

They wait for attention to drift elsewhere. They rely on short memory. They assume pressure will fade. Often, they are right.

Designing pressure that lasts requires a different approach. Campaigns have to be built around actions people can sustain without burning out. That means pacing rather than constant escalation, and repetition rather than permanent urgency. The goal is not to overwhelm opponents in a single surge, but to apply steady, repeatable actions that accumulate effect.

From the outside, effective economic campaigns often look unremarkable. The same demand is repeated. The same actors are named. The same behaviors are monitored over time. This repetition is not a failure of imagination. It is discipline. Consistency is what turns isolated disruption into a recognizable pattern—and patterns are what institutions respond to.

Sustained pressure also depends on feedback. Participants need evidence that their effort is registering, even when outcomes are incremental. A delayed decision, a revised policy, a quiet withdrawal, or a subtle change in language can all serve as signals. These shifts may not feel dramatic, but they matter. They show that pressure is being noticed, and that calculation is beginning to change.

Coordination strengthens this effect. Economic pressure is most effective when actions reinforce one another across domains. Consumer behavior amplifies narrative. Narrative draws regulatory attention. Regulatory attention increases financial risk. None of these elements is sufficient on its own, but together they compound.

Movements often underestimate the importance of pressure short of victory. They assume change only counts when demands are fully met. In practice, partial concessions frequently signal deeper vulnerability. They indicate that pressure is being felt, and that internal reassessment is underway. Those moments are not endpoints—they are openings.

Sustaining pressure also means knowing when not to escalate. Not every moment requires response. Not every provocation demands reply. Strategic patience protects energy and preserves focus. It allows movements to outlast resistance rather than trying to overpower it.

This is where economic strategies align closely with democratic endurance. Authoritarian systems depend on speed and fatigue. Sustained economic pressure slows them down. It introduces friction into systems that rely on smooth, uninterrupted operation.

Economic campaigns succeed when they change the background conditions in which decisions are made—when supporting authoritarian systems begins to feel risky, neutrality becomes costly, and enabling power no longer feels safe. That shift rarely produces dramatic headlines, but it reshapes behavior in durable ways.

In the final section of this chapter, we'll step back and look at how economic pressure fits into the broader democratic strategy this book has been building—how it connects to narrative, culture, and political infrastructure without replacing them. Economic leverage is powerful, but it works best as part of a system.

Section 5

Integrating Economic Pressure Into Democratic Resistance

Economic pressure is powerful, but it is not sufficient on its own. Applied in isolation, it can feel blunt. Used without context, it can feel punitive. Overused, it can provoke backlash or fatigue rather than change. Its real strength lies in how it fits within a larger democratic strategy.

Across this book, a pattern has been taking shape. Narrative work helps people make sense of what is happening. Cultural foundations sustain participation over time. Political infrastructure translates effort into durable constraint. Economic pressure operates alongside these elements, not above them. It reinforces what narrative makes visible, supports what culture holds together, and strengthens what political systems are able to carry forward.

When economic strategies are aligned with narrative, pressure feels legitimate. People understand why certain actors are being targeted and how material relationships connect to democratic harm. Pressure is recognized as accountability rather than punishment. Without that narrative grounding, economic action can appear arbitrary or excessive, even when its aims are justified.

When economic pressure is supported by culture, participation becomes sustainable. People know how to contribute and where they fit. They can engage without constant escalation or urgency. Economic action stops feeling like emergency labor and starts to resemble shared work—something that can be returned to repeatedly without exhaustion.

And when economic pressure connects to political infrastructure, its effects last. Disruption feeds oversight. Oversight informs regulation. Regulation reshapes incentives. What begins as pressure gradually becomes part of the environment in which decisions are made, rather than a temporary interruption.

This integration matters because authoritarian systems adapt. They reroute resources, seek alternative partners, and wait for focus to drift. Isolated tactics are relatively easy to absorb. Integrated strategies are much harder to evade.

In practice, economic pressure works best when it is targeted rather than diffuse, persistent rather than explosive, and coordinated rather than improvised. These qualities mirror the broader democratic approach this book has traced—one oriented toward endurance rather than intensity.

Importantly, economic strategies do not require mass participation to be effective. They depend on coordination among relatively small numbers of people acting deliberately. That makes them especially valuable in environments where large-scale mobilization is difficult or risky. Even when visibility must decrease, resistance can continue.

Economic pressure also stabilizes movements internally. It creates feedback loops and produces measurable outcomes. It grounds effort in tangible consequences rather than abstract hope. That grounding helps prevent drift, burnout, and fragmentation over time.

This chapter has shown how power leaves material traces—and how those traces can be followed, mapped, and pressured. Not to replace democratic institutions, but to protect them. Not to escalate conflict, but to introduce limits where none exist.

In the chapters that follow, the focus shifts again. From systems to practice. From strategy to habit. From pressure points to participation over time. Because resistance that endures is not built on moments. It is built on routines people can live with—day after day, even when progress is slow.

Section 6

What This Looks Like

When the economic battlefield becomes visible, resistance stops feeling abstract. Not because people suddenly understand finance or corporate structure in detail, but because power begins to appear as something that moves through ordinary systems rather than hovering above them.

In practice, this often starts quietly. Someone notices a repeated name attached to contracts, services, or funding streams. Someone else recognizes that the same intermediary appears across different institutions. Over time, patterns emerge—not dramatic revelations, but accumulations of attention. Power becomes traceable rather than assumed.

Economic resistance at this level rarely looks confrontational. It looks like sustained noticing. The same relationships are named consistently. The same questions are asked again and again. Who insures this? Who underwrites it? Who benefits if nothing changes? These questions do not accuse. They clarify. And clarity itself begins to exert pressure.

Participation in this work does not require mass mobilization. It often involves relatively small groups of people dividing attention rather than concentrating it. One person tracks disclosures. Another monitors public statements. Another pays attention to regulatory signals. No one is expected to master the entire system. The work persists because responsibility is distributed and bounded.

Pressure, when it is applied, feels deliberate rather than explosive. Targets are chosen not for visibility, but for sensitivity. The same demand is repeated calmly over time. The same relationship is brought into focus across different contexts. The effect is cumulative. Risk calculations shift gradually—not because of outrage, but because uncertainty settles in.

This kind of economic pressure often produces subtle changes before obvious ones. Language softens. Decisions are delayed. Partnerships quietly dissolve. These shifts can be easy to miss, especially for participants expecting decisive moments. But they matter. They indicate that the system is no longer moving frictionlessly.

Importantly, this work does not replace other forms of engagement. It reinforces them. Narrative explains why pressure exists. Culture sustains participation when outcomes are slow. Political infrastructure ensures that changes, once made, are not easily reversed. Economic pressure adds constraint where persuasion alone cannot.

What is absent here is just as important. There is no demand for constant escalation. No expectation that every enabling relationship must be confronted at once. No belief that pressure only counts if it is public or dramatic. Economic resistance relies on persistence, not spectacle.

Over time, this changes how authoritarian systems operate. Support becomes more cautious. Neutrality becomes less comfortable. Enabling power carries cost rather than convenience. None of this happens all at once. But momentum slows, options narrow, and consolidation becomes harder to sustain.

This is what it means to engage the economic battlefield without becoming consumed by it. Not by matching power with power, but by introducing friction where smooth operation is assumed. Not by heroic disruption, but by sustained attention that does not fade when headlines move on.

In the next chapter, the focus shifts again—from systems of power to the people who inhabit them. Because even the most effective strategies fail if participation cannot be carried forward over time. Endurance, once again, becomes the measure of success.

CHAPTER 8
Converting the Passive Enablers

Section 1

The Quiet Majority That Sustains Power

When Václav Havel wrote *The Power of the Powerless*, he was not trying to explain tyranny by pointing to its loudest supporters. He was trying to understand everyone else.

He described a system sustained less by belief than by habit. Shopkeepers who displayed party slogans they did not believe. Citizens who repeated phrases they did not endorse. People who complied not because they were convinced, but because compliance felt easier than standing out. Havel's insight was unsettling precisely because it was ordinary: authoritarian systems do not survive on enthusiasm alone. They survive on accommodation.

The people he described were not villains. They were not ideologues. They were trying to get through their days without inviting trouble. And in doing so, they became something both smaller and more powerful than supporters: they became stabilizers. They allowed the system to function without needing constant force.

This pattern appears again and again across authoritarian contexts. Power consolidates not because most people want it, but because many decide that resistance feels too costly, too risky, or too uncertain. Over time, non-participation begins to function like consent. Silence becomes infrastructure.

This is the group most resistance movements misunderstand. They are often described as apathetic, cowardly, or morally compromised. But those labels obscure what actually matters. Passive enablers are rarely committed to authoritarian outcomes. They are committed to continuity. To protecting their families. Their livelihoods. Their sense of normalcy. They calculate—often accurately—that confrontation carries immediate costs, while accommodation appears manageable.

That calculation is not made once. It is made repeatedly. Every day that passes without overt catastrophe reinforces it.

What matters strategically is this: authoritarian systems do not need to persuade this group. They only need to keep it from moving. As long as the middle remains inert—neither resisting nor organizing—power can advance with relatively little opposition.

This is why resistance efforts that focus primarily on confronting extremists so often stall. The loudest supporters are rarely the leverage point. The decisive terrain lies with those who are uneasy, unconvinced, and still weighing their options.

This chapter is about that terrain. Not how to shame it. Not how to bypass it. But how to understand it well enough to engage it differently. Because history is remarkably consistent on this point: durable resistance does not begin by converting the most committed authoritarians. It begins by activating the people who have not yet chosen a side—and who are quietly holding the system in place by waiting.

Section 2

Obedience Without Belief

One of the most persistent myths about authoritarian systems is that they depend on belief. That people comply because they are convinced, indoctrinated, or ideologically aligned. In reality, belief is often incidental. What sustains authoritarian power far more reliably is obedience without belief.

This distinction matters because it changes where resistance focuses its energy. If power depended primarily on conviction, counter-arguments and exposure might be enough. But obedience does not require agreement. It only requires behavior.

Psychologists began studying this gap between belief and action long before modern authoritarianism took its current form. The most famous experiments showed that ordinary people could be induced to carry out harmful actions even while privately objecting to them. Participants were not sadists. They were not committed to the authority issuing the instructions. Many expressed discomfort, hesitation, and even distress. And yet, they continued.

What allowed that continuation was not ideology. It was context. Authority was framed as legitimate. Responsibility was displaced upward. Consequences were normalized as part of a process rather than a personal choice. Participants were not asked to commit to cruelty. They were asked to follow instructions, step by step, in a setting designed to feel routine and official.

Authoritarian systems scale this dynamic. They create environments where compliance feels procedural rather than moral. Where actions are framed as requirements rather than choices. Where responsibility appears diffused across roles, departments, or rules. People are not asked to endorse repression. They are asked to do their jobs. To follow policy. To avoid making trouble.

Over time, this produces a dangerous psychological shift. People begin to separate what they think from what they do. Private discomfort coexists with public compliance. And because nothing dramatic happens at first, that separation feels manageable. This is how systems become normalized without ever being embraced.

Another key factor is gradualism. Authoritarian power rarely demands everything at once. It advances in increments small enough to rationalize. Each step feels tolerable in isolation. Each adjustment appears temporary, or technical, or necessary given the circumstances. Resistance feels disproportionate to the offense. Silence feels reasonable.

But each step resets the baseline. What once would have felt unacceptable becomes familiar. What once triggered debate becomes procedure. People adapt not because they agree, but because adaptation feels easier than disruption. And once adaptation becomes habitual, reversing it begins to feel risky.

This is why moral appeals often fail to move passive enablers. They already know something is wrong. What they lack is not awareness, but a viable alternative that does not require individual sacrifice without collective support.

Obedience without belief thrives in isolation. People comply more readily when they believe they are alone in their doubts. When dissent feels singular, costly, or futile. Authoritarian systems reinforce this perception by fragmenting opposition and keeping discomfort private.

Which leads to a crucial implication for resistance. If obedience is sustained by context rather than conviction, then resistance must focus on changing context. Not by demanding purity or courage from isolated individuals, but by altering the environment in which decisions are made. Making dissent visible. Making participation shared. Making non-compliance less lonely and less risky.

The goal is not to persuade everyone to believe differently. It is to interrupt routines that allow people to act against their own values without feeling responsible for the outcome.

In the next section, we'll look at how authoritarian systems deliberately engineer those routines—how bureaucracy, procedure, and institutional design are used to transform personal hesitation into collective compliance.

Because power rarely advances by force alone. It advances by making obedience feel ordinary.

Section 3
How Systems Make Compliance Ordinary

Authoritarian power becomes durable not when people agree with it, but when compliance feels routine. The most effective systems do not rely on constant coercion. They rely on design—on environments that make certain behaviors feel normal, expected, and unremarkable.

Bureaucracy plays a central role in this process. Rules, forms, procedures, and protocols create distance between individual action and collective outcome. When harm is produced through a chain of small, compartmentalized decisions, no single person feels responsible for the result. Each actor handles only a fragment. Accountability dissolves into process.

This is not unique to authoritarian states. Large organizations everywhere depend on compartmentalization. But authoritarian systems exploit it deliberately.

They structure institutions so that morally consequential decisions are broken into administratively neutral tasks. People are not asked to commit injustices. They are asked to process requests, enforce guidelines, or implement policy.

Language matters here. Words like "compliance," "security," "efficiency," and "risk management" replace moral vocabulary. Actions that would provoke ethical resistance if described plainly are reframed as technical necessities. Over time, this linguistic shift changes how people interpret their own behavior. What might once have felt like a choice begins to feel like an obligation.

Another mechanism is predictability. Systems reward those who follow procedure and penalize those who deviate. Careers advance through reliability rather than judgment. Questioning slows operations and introduces uncertainty. Silence, by contrast, is efficient. In such environments, conformity does not require belief. It requires only an understanding of incentives.

Gradual escalation further reinforces this pattern. Policies tighten incrementally. Oversight expands step by step. Each change is small enough to justify on its own. People adapt not because they approve, but because adaptation feels easier than confrontation. Once routines adjust, earlier norms fade from memory.

What makes this especially powerful is that compliance becomes social. When everyone around you follows the same procedures, deviation feels abnormal. Risk concentrates on the dissenter rather than the system. Over time, people internalize the idea that resistance is disruptive, unprofessional, or naïve.

This is how moral discomfort is managed. Instead of being resolved, it is absorbed into routine. People learn to separate personal values from institutional roles. They tell themselves that responsibility lies elsewhere—with policymakers, leaders, or abstract forces beyond their control.

The result is a system that functions smoothly even as it produces outcomes many participants privately oppose. Power advances without spectacle. Harm occurs without obvious villains. And because everything appears orderly, opposition struggles to find traction.

For resistance, this presents a challenge and an opportunity. If compliance is produced by ordinary routines, then it can also be disrupted by altering those routines. Making procedures visible. Reconnecting actions to consequences. Creating shared moments of refusal that break the illusion of inevitability.

In the next section, we'll examine how authoritarian systems respond when compliance wavers—how they manage dissent not primarily through repression, but through isolation, uncertainty, and selective punishment. Because the goal is rarely to crush opposition outright. It is to make resistance feel abnormal, risky, and unsustainable.

Section 4

How Dissent Is Isolated

When compliance begins to feel ordinary, authoritarian systems do not need to eliminate dissent entirely. They only need to prevent it from becoming collective. Isolated dissent is manageable. Coordinated dissent is dangerous. The difference between the two determines whether resistance fades quietly or gains momentum.

One of the most effective tools for isolating dissent is uncertainty. Rules are applied inconsistently. Boundaries are left vague. Consequences are unpredictable. People are never quite sure which actions will trigger retaliation and which will be ignored. This ambiguity encourages self-censorship. When the risks are unclear, caution feels prudent.

Selective enforcement plays a similar role. A few visible penalties—an investigation, a demotion, a public rebuke—send a signal far beyond the individuals directly affected. Others adjust their behavior without needing to be told. The system does not have to punish everyone. It only has to make an example of some.

Importantly, this isolation is often social rather than physical. Dissenters are portrayed as disruptive, irresponsible, or disloyal. Their motives are questioned. Their credibility is undermined. They are framed as exceptions rather than indicators of a broader problem. Over time, people learn that speaking up carries reputational costs even when formal protections remain intact.

Authoritarian systems also exploit fragmentation. Different groups are encouraged to see their concerns as separate and competing. Workers, professionals, activists, and public servants experience pressure in different ways and at different times. Without shared forums or coordinated action, each group feels alone in its struggle. Isolation becomes structural.

Another subtle mechanism is exhaustion through process. Complaints are routed through slow, opaque channels. Appeals are delayed. Procedures multiply. Nothing is resolved quickly. People who raise concerns spend enormous energy navigating bureaucracy, while those who remain silent move on with their lives. Over time, dissent begins to feel inefficient.

The cumulative effect is psychological. People start to doubt whether resistance is worth the cost. They tell themselves that others are not willing to take the same risks. Silence appears rational. Participation feels lonely. The possibility of collective action recedes.

What matters most here is that repression is rarely total. Formal freedoms often remain on paper. Speech is not banned outright. Protest is not always prohibited. But the environment is shaped so that exercising those freedoms feels isolating and unsustainable. The system maintains plausible deniability while achieving its goal.

For resistance movements, this means that courage alone is not enough. Individual acts of defiance, however principled, can be neutralized if they remain isolated. What changes the equation is visibility and coordination—making dissent legible as shared rather than singular.

In the next section, we'll look at how authoritarian systems use time itself as a weapon—how delay, distraction, and constant crisis prevent opposition from consolidating even when dissent is widespread. Because power is not only exercised through force or fear. It is exercised through tempo.

Section 5

Time as a Weapon

Authoritarian systems rarely rush to finish the work of consolidation. They stretch it out. Time becomes an instrument of control—not by speeding events up, but by managing when attention is required and when it is allowed to fade.

One way this happens is through delay. Investigations are opened but never concluded. Reviews are announced but not completed. Reforms are proposed, revised, and postponed. Each step signals responsiveness while quietly draining urgency. People wait for outcomes that never arrive, and waiting becomes a substitute for action.

At the same time, crises are layered. Just as attention begins to settle on one issue, another emerges. Scandals overlap. Conflicts multiply. Nothing is resolved cleanly. The result is not confusion alone, but fatigue. People struggle to maintain focus when there is no sense of progress or closure.

This constant motion creates a psychological trap. When events move too quickly, people feel overwhelmed. When they move too slowly, people disengage. Authoritarian systems alternate between these extremes, keeping opposition off balance. Reflection is crowded out by reaction, and long-term strategy gives way to short-term coping.

Another effect of delay is normalization. What remains unresolved long enough begins to feel permanent. Temporary measures lose their provisional status. Emergency powers persist. Unusual arrangements become familiar. Over time, people stop asking when things will return to normal and start adjusting their expectations to what is.

This adjustment is rarely conscious. It happens through repetition. Each day that passes without reversal lowers the emotional charge of earlier violations. Outrage softens into resignation. What once demanded resistance begins to feel like background conditions of life.

Authoritarian systems benefit enormously from this shift. They do not need to convince people that changes are good. They only need people to accept that they are lasting. Once that acceptance sets in, resistance feels belated and impractical. Acting later appears riskier than acting earlier, and earlier opportunities feel irretrievable.

The manipulation of time also fragments opposition. Different groups respond to different moments. Some mobilize early and burn out. Others wait for clearer signals and arrive late. Without shared pacing, coordination weakens. Each group feels out of sync with the others.

For resistance movements, this reveals an important lesson. Power is not exercised only through decisions and policies. It is exercised through tempo. Who sets the pace determines who must react. And those who are always reacting rarely control outcomes.

Interrupting this dynamic requires reclaiming time. Creating rhythms of engagement that are not dictated by crisis. Building structures that allow participation to continue even when headlines move on. Designing action that compounds rather than resets with each new event.

In the next section of this chapter, we'll look at where this entire system becomes vulnerable—where dependence on isolation, exhaustion, and time management begins to strain. Because the same mechanisms that stabilize authoritarian power also limit it. And those limits are where durable resistance finds its footing.

Section 6

Where Ordinary Power Breaks

Authoritarian systems often appear strongest when resistance feels weakest.

Compliance seems widespread. Dissent appears isolated. Time stretches on without resolution. From the outside, the system looks settled. But this stability is more fragile than it appears.

The same mechanisms that make authoritarian power durable also constrain it. Systems built on routine compliance require constant maintenance. They depend on people continuing to act in ways they do not fully endorse. They rely on silence remaining easier than participation, and withdrawal remaining safer than engagement. When those conditions change, even slightly, the system begins to strain.

One vulnerability lies in coordination. Authoritarian power is effective when opposition is fragmented and asynchronous. But when people begin to see their hesitation reflected in others—when private doubts become visible and shared—compliance loses its inevitability. What felt like personal caution begins to look like collective delay. And delay can be reversed.

Another vulnerability lies in overextension. Systems that rely on constant crisis, selective enforcement, and procedural complexity generate their own inefficiencies. Decisions bottleneck. Information degrades. Loyalty replaces competence. Over time, the system becomes less adaptive, not more. What once felt controlled begins to feel brittle.

There is also a deeper contradiction. Authoritarian systems demand obedience but cannot generate trust. Fear enforces behavior, but it corrodes initiative. People comply, but they stop contributing honestly. Problems are hidden. Errors compound. Leaders receive filtered information that confirms expectations rather than challenges them. This is why such systems often appear confident until they suddenly falter.

Most importantly, authoritarian power depends on passivity, not belief. People do not need to agree. They only need to disengage. Which means that engagement—when it becomes shared, visible, and sustained—creates pressure the system is poorly equipped to handle. Not all at once, and not dramatically, but measurably.

This is where many accounts of authoritarianism stop, as if diagnosis were the same as inevitability. It isn't. What matters is not overthrowing power in a single moment, but interrupting its momentum. Slowing consolidation. Raising costs. Creating friction where routines once ran smoothly.

That kind of resistance does not look heroic. It does not rely on constant protest or moral intensity. It relies on design. On structures that reduce isolation. On roles that distribute responsibility. On rhythms that make participation repeatable rather than exhausting.

This chapter has shown how ordinary behavior sustains extraordinary outcomes. How systems endure not through fanaticism, but through routine. The chapters that follow turn fully toward what changes that equation. How resistance can be built to last. How participation can become manageable rather than overwhelming. And how people who are not heroes, not extremists, and not always brave can nonetheless interrupt authoritarian momentum—together. Because the strongest challenge to authoritarian power is not outrage. It is organized persistence.

Section 7

What This Looks Like

Converting passive enablers rarely looks like persuading someone in a dramatic conversation. More often, it looks like changing what feels normal around them.

In practice, passive enabling is sustained by a quiet calculation: If I keep my head down, nothing bad happens to me. The goal is not to insult that calculation or demand bravery. The goal is to alter the environment so that keeping one's head down no longer feels like the safest, easiest option—and so that small acts of participation feel less lonely and less risky.

This begins with visibility. Passive enablers often assume they are alone in their discomfort. They suspect something is wrong, but they do not see others naming it calmly, consistently, and without hysteria. When doubts remain private, obedience remains easy. When doubts become legible—when people realize others share the same hesitation—compliance loses some of its emotional protection.

That visibility does not require confrontation. Often it comes through simple, repeated signals that break the illusion of unanimity: someone refusing to repeat a phrase they do not believe; someone asking a procedural question that reconnects policy to consequence; someone naming a change as a choice rather than a necessity. These are not dramatic acts. But they interrupt routine, and routine is where obedience lives.

Conversion also happens when participation becomes low-risk and distributed. Passive enablers do not need to be asked for transformation. They need an entry point that does not expose them to immediate social or professional loss. In practice, this means spaces where observation is allowed, where contribution can be partial, and where people can move closer without being forced to declare identity. The first step is often not public dissent. It is private alignment with a shared structure.

Another shift comes from role clarity. Passive enabling thrives when responsibility is vague: It's not my job. Someone else decides. The rules require it. When roles are defined in ways that reconnect action to consequence, people have a place to stand. Not a heroic stance. A functional one. It becomes easier to say, This is the part I won't do, or This is the question I will keep asking, because the burden is limited and the boundary is clear.

Time is the other lever. Authoritarian systems rely on people waiting—waiting for courts, waiting for elections, waiting for investigations, waiting for normal to return. Conversion often begins when people stop waiting for closure and start adopting a rhythm that does not depend on headlines. Not constant intensity, but repeatable presence. The same question asked again. The same oversight maintained. The same small refusal repeated. This is how people move from private discomfort to public steadiness without making a single dramatic leap.

What changes passive enablers is rarely moral pressure. Many already feel the moral weight. What they lack is a credible path that does not demand solitary sacrifice. They need proof that participation is shared, that risk is distributed, that absence is survivable, and that the work will continue even if they are not extraordinary.

When those conditions exist, conversion becomes less psychological and more structural. People begin to participate not because they have become braver, but because the environment has changed. Silence is no longer the default. Compliance no longer feels merely procedural. Waiting no longer feels like neutrality. And the middle—once inert—begins to move.

This is the fragile point where ordinary power starts to strain. Not because the loudest supporters have been defeated, but because the quiet stabilizers begin, gradually, to withdraw their accommodation. Organized persistence replaces isolated discomfort. And that is where authoritarian momentum slows.

Converting The Passive Enablers

CHAPTER 9
Activating the Disengaged

Section 1

Activating the Disengaged

Up to this point, this book has focused on groups that remain politically adjacent: active defenders of democracy and those who enable erosion through accommodation or rationalization. But there is a larger group whose absence shapes outcomes just as decisively. These are people who are not watching, not choosing sides, and not participating at all.

Disengagement is often misunderstood. It is treated as apathy, ignorance, or indifference. In reality, disengagement is usually the result of experience. People withdraw not because they lack opinions, but because they have learned—sometimes repeatedly—that participation carries cost without reward. Over time, disengagement becomes a rational response to systems perceived as unresponsive, extractive, or closed.

This distinction matters because strategies that work for persuading passive enablers often fail entirely with the disengaged. Passive enablers still see themselves as political actors. They follow events. They vote intermittently. They argue, justify, and rationalize. The disengaged do not. Appeals that rely on moral pressure, ideological framing, or calls to responsibility often miss them completely, because those appeals assume a civic identity that no longer feels available.

For democratic movements, this creates a structural problem. Disengaged populations are often large, demographically diverse, and unevenly distributed across regions. Their absence lowers participation thresholds for authoritarian minorities and reduces the legitimacy of democratic institutions. Yet traditional mobilization tactics—awareness campaigns, messaging, voter reminders—tend to have limited impact, precisely because they address symptoms rather than causes.

The central insight of this chapter is that disengagement is not primarily an attitudinal failure. It is a structural and experiential one. People disengage when political systems feel distant, symbolic, or irrelevant to their daily lives. They re-engage only when participation becomes tangible, legible, and connected to outcomes they can observe.

This means that activating the disengaged is not about intensifying persuasion. It is about redesigning entry points into civic life. Instead of asking people to care more, effective movements reduce the cost of caring. Instead of demanding belief, they offer participation that produces visible consequence. Instead of treating disengagement as a deficit, they treat it as a signal.

The sections that follow examine how this works in practice. They focus on the specific barriers that separate disengagement from passive enablement, and on the design principles that allow people with no active civic identity to take initial steps toward participation. Not through urgency or fear, but through relevance and credibility.

Because democratic renewal does not begin by convincing everyone. It begins by making participation possible again for people who have learned—often correctly—that it was not.

Section 2

Moving from Awareness to Action

The first challenge in activating disengaged people is not getting them to notice a problem. Many already do. They see instability, unfairness, and erosion clearly enough. What's missing is not awareness, but a credible path from recognition to participation.

Disengagement often forms when people learn that attention does not lead to impact. They may follow events closely for a time, feel concern, even anger, and still conclude that acting will not change outcomes in any meaningful way. Over time, that conclusion hardens. Awareness becomes passive. Concern becomes background noise.

This is why appeals that work with politically adjacent groups fail here. Moral urgency, ideological framing, or calls to civic duty assume that people already see themselves as participants. The disengaged often do not. They don't feel inside the system, and they don't believe the system responds to them. Asking them to care more simply increases distance.

What changes behavior is not intensity of message, but clarity of action. People begin to re-engage when they can see what participation looks like, what it costs, and what it produces. Not in theory, but in practice. When the first step is concrete, limited, and legible, it becomes possible to take without reordering one's identity.

This means that effective activation does not begin with argument. It begins with design. The first invitation into participation has to feel safe enough to try, ordinary enough to repeat, and meaningful enough to justify the effort. When engagement requires fluency, certainty, or public performance, it quietly excludes those who have already learned to stay away.

Urgency still matters, but it has to be calibrated. Permanent emergency produces avoidance, not commitment. People shut down when the message suggests endless strain without agency. What works better is bounded urgency: a clear problem paired with a clear, time-limited action that visibly contributes to a larger effort. Pressure without paralysis.

Another critical shift is moving from abstraction to lived experience. Many disengaged people do not respond to democratic ideals because those ideals feel distant from their daily lives. Participation begins to make sense when political systems are shown to intersect directly with health, work, housing, safety, and dignity. Democracy becomes relevant not as a moral demand, but as a tool that can be used.

Taken together, these dynamics point to a simple conclusion. Disengagement is not a lack of values. It is a learned response to systems that have felt unresponsive or inaccessible. Re-engagement begins when participation is redesigned to meet people where they are, rather than where movements wish they were.

The next section builds on this foundation by asking a harder question: once someone takes a first step back into civic life, what allows that step to become a path instead of a one-time exception?

Section 3

Designing First Steps That Stick

For disengaged people, the first act of participation is the most fragile. It carries the highest uncertainty and the lowest confidence of return. If that initial experience feels confusing, ineffective, or socially risky, it confirms the lesson that led to withdrawal in the first place. Re-engagement fails not because people are unwilling, but because the first step does not hold.

This is why the design of early participation matters more than its scale. Large asks, public declarations, or identity-laden commitments raise the cost of entry and narrow the pool of people willing to try. For someone who has learned to stay away from politics, these demands feel premature. They require belief before experience, and loyalty before trust.

What works better are roles that are concrete and limited. Tasks that are easy to understand, bounded in time, and clearly connected to a visible outcome. When people can see what they are doing, why it matters, and when it ends, participation becomes manageable rather than overwhelming. The goal of early engagement is not intensity. It is repeatability.

Another key element is social reinforcement. Disengaged people are more likely to return when participation creates connection rather than exposure. Small group settings, shared tasks, and informal collaboration reduce the sense of risk. They replace performance with contribution. When people feel useful rather than judged, confidence grows naturally.

This is also where many movements unintentionally fail. They treat the first step as a filter rather than a bridge. Language assumes prior knowledge. Norms go unstated. Mistakes are corrected publicly. The message becomes clear without being spoken: this space is for people who already know how to be here. Those who don't quietly disappear.

Designing first steps that stick requires reversing that logic. Participation has to teach people how to participate. It has to build skill and confidence gradually, without demanding fluency or certainty at the outset. Early involvement should feel like learning, not auditioning.

Time also plays a role. When participation is episodic or crisis-driven, re-engagement becomes harder. People who step in once have no clear way to step in again. Durable engagement depends on rhythm. Predictable opportunities, familiar roles, and visible continuity allow people to integrate participation into ordinary life instead of treating it as an exception.

The result of this kind of design is not instant mobilization. It is something quieter and more durable. People begin to see themselves as capable participants. They develop a sense of efficacy grounded in experience rather than belief. Over time, disengagement gives way not to constant activism, but to steady involvement.

The next section examines how these individual pathways connect to something larger. How early participation scales without becoming extractive. And how movements can grow without recreating the very barriers that produced disengagement in the first place.

Section 4

Scaling Without Recreating Disengagement

One of the most common mistakes movements make after successfully re-engaging people is assuming that what worked at the beginning will work indefinitely. Early participation is designed to lower barriers, reduce risk, and build confidence. But if growth is handled poorly, scale can recreate the same distance and inefficacy that caused disengagement in the first place.

As participation expands, coordination becomes more complex. New roles emerge. Decisions take longer. Informal norms harden into expectations. Without care, early contributors begin to feel replaceable or invisible. The sense that effort matters—so critical in initial engagement—starts to erode. When that happens, disengagement does not announce itself. It quietly returns.

This is why scaling participation is not simply a matter of adding more people. It requires maintaining legibility. People need to understand how their contribution fits into the larger effort, even as the effort grows. When the system becomes opaque—when outcomes feel distant or decisions feel inaccessible—participation slips back into abstraction.

Another risk emerges around centralization. As movements grow, authority often concentrates for the sake of efficiency. This can be necessary. But when decision-making becomes disconnected from contribution, people revert to spectator roles. They may still show up occasionally, but their sense of agency diminishes. Participation becomes symbolic rather than consequential.

Effective scaling preserves pathways rather than flattening them. New participants should be able to see where they are, where they could go next, and how deeper involvement works. Growth should expand opportunity, not narrow it. When people can imagine themselves continuing, they are more likely to stay.

Communication also changes at scale. Messages that once traveled through conversation and shared experience now move through platforms and broadcasts. This increases reach, but it can weaken trust. Disengaged people are especially sensitive to messaging that feels generic or performative. If communication becomes detached from lived experience, credibility erodes.

What prevents this is feedback. Visible response to participation. Evidence that actions register. Signals that adjustment is possible. When people see that engagement still influences direction—even imperfectly—they remain invested. When feedback disappears, participation becomes hollow.

Scaling that works does not chase constant expansion. It stabilizes before it grows. It protects coherence. It resists the pressure to substitute numbers for depth.

Most importantly, it treats disengagement not as a failure of commitment, but as a design signal that something essential has been lost.

The final section of this chapter turns to what happens when these design principles hold over time. How disengaged people move from tentative involvement to durable participation. And how democratic engagement becomes something people can sustain—not as an emergency response, but as part of ordinary life.

Section 5

From Participation to Persistence

Re-engagement succeeds only when it lasts. A single action, even a positive one, does not reverse disengagement. What changes people's relationship to civic life is repetition—participation that becomes familiar, manageable, and worth returning to.

Persistence depends less on motivation than on conditions. People continue showing up when engagement fits into their lives without constant strain. When participation requires sustained urgency, emotional intensity, or personal sacrifice, it eventually collapses. This is not a failure of character. It is a mismatch between human limits and movement design.

Durable participation is built through rhythm. Predictable moments of involvement. Clear expectations about time and effort. Roles that remain stable long enough to feel competent in, but flexible enough to adjust as life changes. When engagement has a rhythm, people stop asking whether they can afford to participate. It becomes something they plan around rather than decide anew each time.

Another condition for persistence is visible accumulation. People need to see that small actions add up. Not necessarily to dramatic victories, but to incremental change: a policy delayed, a practice altered, a decision scrutinized more closely than before. These signals anchor effort in reality. They counter the learned belief that participation disappears into a void.

Social continuity matters as well. Disengagement often thrives in isolation. Persistence grows in relationship. When people recognize others over time—when participation creates familiarity rather than anonymity—commitment deepens naturally. Belonging does not need to be declared. It emerges through shared work.

Movements undermine persistence when they constantly reset. New campaigns, new language, new priorities appear before participants have time to integrate what they've already done. This can feel energizing from the center, but disorienting at the edges. People who are just finding their footing lose it again.

Designing for persistence means valuing continuity over novelty. Protecting existing pathways. Letting people stay in roles long enough to feel capable. Allowing contribution to evolve gradually rather than demanding reinvention. These choices may feel slow, but they are what turn participation into habit.

This is where disengagement truly breaks. Not through persuasion or pressure, but through experience. People stop seeing civic life as something they visit occasionally and start experiencing it as something they inhabit. Not constantly. Not heroically. But reliably.

The chapter closes by returning to the broader argument of the book. Democratic defense does not require awakening everyone or sustaining perpetual mobilization. It requires enough people re-engaging in ways they can live with, long enough to interrupt authoritarian momentum. That work begins with design, not demand.

Section 6

What Re-Engagement Makes Possible

Disengagement is often treated as the end of the story. Once people withdraw, it is assumed they are lost—unreachable, uninterested, or permanently alienated. This chapter has argued something different. Disengagement is not a fixed trait. It is a condition produced by experience, structure, and design. And what is produced can be altered.

Re-engagement does not require transformation. It does not depend on people becoming more virtuous, informed, or politically sophisticated. It depends on whether participation becomes intelligible again—whether it feels connected to outcomes, shared with others, and sustainable over time.

When disengaged people begin to return, even modestly, the effects compound. Not because every participant becomes deeply involved, but because the environment shifts. Silence no longer feels universal. Withdrawal no longer appears inevitable. What once felt like a private decision begins to look like a collective pattern that can be interrupted.

This is where authoritarian systems feel pressure they are poorly designed to manage. They rely on disengagement to keep resistance fragmented and invisible. When people re-enter civic life in coordinated, persistent ways—without spectacle, without constant outrage—the system's assumptions begin to fail. Decisions attract scrutiny. Procedures slow. Costs rise.

Importantly, this does not require mass conversion or constant mobilization. It requires enough people engaging consistently enough to change the background conditions under which power operates. Re-engagement restores friction. And friction is what prevents consolidation.

This also clarifies a recurring mistake in democratic strategy. The goal is not to "activate everyone." It is to make participation normal again for people who learned that it was pointless. When engagement becomes routine rather than exceptional, democratic defense stops depending on moments of crisis and starts relying on continuity.

What re-engagement ultimately makes possible is not victory, but durability. The capacity to persist without burning out. The ability to respond without panic. The strength to act even when progress is slow and incomplete.

That is the thread connecting this chapter to what follows. Re-engagement is not the end of the work. It is the condition that allows the rest of the work to happen.

The next chapter turns from individuals back to systems—specifically, how re-engaged participation reshapes the economic, cultural, and political terrain on which democratic resistance either falters or holds. Because disengagement is not only a personal withdrawal. It is a structural vulnerability. And once addressed, it becomes a structural strength.

Section 7

What This Looks Like

Activating the disengaged rarely looks like waking people up. Most are not asleep. They are overloaded, skeptical, and tired of paying attention without seeing anything change.

In practice, re-engagement begins when participation stops feeling like an identity and starts feeling like a small, bounded act that has a visible shape. Someone is not asked to "get involved." They are invited into something they can understand quickly, do without exposure, and finish without being trapped. The first step is not a declaration. It is an experience.

Often the turning point is not persuasion but credibility. A disengaged person is watching for signs that the invitation is real: that the ask is limited, the time is respected, and the outcome is not imaginary. They return when they feel their effort landed somewhere—when the action connects to a consequence, even a modest one. Not a victory, necessarily. A signal that participation does not disappear.

Re-engagement also looks socially different than most movements expect. Disengaged people rarely want to enter a space where language is specialized, norms are implicit, or disagreement feels unsafe. They move toward settings that feel ordinary: small groups, concrete tasks, familiar faces, low drama. The work is not staged. It resembles life. This is where people can re-learn civic presence without feeling evaluated.

Early participation that sticks tends to be repetitive rather than inspiring. It shows up as a rhythm: a predictable moment of involvement, a role that stays stable long enough to feel competent in, a simple way to step in again without renegotiating everything. People do not "decide to re-engage" anew each time. They begin to plan around the rhythm. That is the moment disengagement starts to break.

At scale, the difference is felt in legibility. People can see where they are in the effort and what their contribution connects to. They do not need to understand the whole system. They need to understand their part. When movements keep that legibility, growth does not recreate distance. When they lose it, even well-intentioned expansion starts to feel like the same old extraction: more attention demanded, more urgency, less agency.

Re-engagement also changes what politics feels like. The disengaged are often repelled by permanent crisis, constant moral performance, and endless argument. When participation is designed to endure, the emotional texture shifts. Less adrenaline. Less spectacle. More steadiness. That steadiness is not boring in a bad way—it is relief. It makes the work survivable.

Over time, the effect compounds quietly. A disengaged person who takes one bounded step and then another does not become a hero. They become present. Their presence changes the environment around them. Silence stops feeling universal. Withdrawal stops feeling inevitable. Participation begins to look like something ordinary people can do without giving up their lives.

This is what successful activation looks like. Not mass awakening. Not constant mobilization. A gradual re-normalization of civic life—where showing up becomes routine enough that it no longer requires special motivation.

And when that happens at meaningful scale, authoritarian momentum slows for a simple reason: disengagement is one of its most reliable allies. When people re-enter shared participation—calmly, repeatedly, without spectacle—power loses one of the conditions it depends on.

The next chapter turns from individuals to the systems that have to hold them. Because re-engagement is not only a personal shift. It becomes a structural force only when it is supported by institutions, roles, and routines that can carry participation forward.

CHAPTER 10
Local Power Building

Section 1

When Institutions Become the Battleground

When democratic systems come under sustained pressure, attention often focuses on elections, leaders, and public opinion. These are visible arenas where conflict plays out dramatically. But long before democracy collapses—or survives—its fate is often decided elsewhere, inside institutions.

Courts, regulatory agencies, civil services, school boards, professional bodies, and administrative offices rarely attract mass attention, and they almost never inspire protest. Yet they are where democratic rules are interpreted, enforced, delayed, or quietly ignored. They are where abstract principles become operational reality.

This is why authoritarian movements invest so much effort here. Not because institutions are glamorous, but because they are decisive. Control of institutions allows power to persist even when public support wavers. It allows leaders to govern through procedure rather than persuasion. And it allows erosion to occur without spectacle.

Democracy depends on institutions doing something very specific: applying rules consistently, even when doing so is inconvenient or politically costly. That consistency is what turns laws into limits rather than suggestions. When institutions stop functioning this way, democratic safeguards weaken even if democratic language remains intact.

What makes this especially dangerous is how normal it looks from the outside. Institutions are not abolished. Offices remain staffed. Meetings continue. Paperwork flows. From a distance, everything appears stable. But internally, priorities shift. Enforcement becomes selective. Professional judgment narrows. Independence erodes without being formally revoked.

Most people experience this change indirectly, if at all. A delayed decision. A rule applied unevenly. A complaint quietly dismissed. Each instance feels isolated, technical, and hard to interpret. And because institutions are complex by design, it is easy to assume someone else understands what is happening better than you do.

Authoritarian systems rely on this opacity. They do not need people to approve of institutional capture. They only need people to disengage from it. When procedures feel too technical to follow and too boring to contest, accountability weakens and power gains room to consolidate.

This chapter is about shifting attention to that terrain. Not to turn everyone into an expert. Not to demand constant vigilance. But to understand why institutions matter so deeply to democratic survival—and why resistance that ignores them remains vulnerable, no matter how passionate or widespread it becomes.

In the sections that follow, we'll examine how institutions are pressured, reshaped, and repurposed over time. How independence is narrowed without open confrontation. And how ordinary people, acting collectively and deliberately, can still exert influence in systems designed to feel unreachable.

Because democracy does not collapse only when people stop voting. It collapses when institutions stop holding.

Section 2

How Institutions Are Quietly Bent

Institutional capture tends to happen through small procedural changes that accumulate over time, often without drawing much attention when they occur. Nothing dramatic announces the shift. The system continues to function while its internal balance slowly changes.

Rules are not discarded outright. They are reinterpreted. Procedures remain in place, but expectations around how they are applied begin to drift. Decisions that once required explanation begin to move forward with less scrutiny. Each change appears technical, even reasonable, when viewed on its own. What alters the system is the accumulation.

In local government, this often becomes visible first in places few people regularly watch. A school board quietly revises how curriculum challenges are handled, narrowing the window for public input. A city council adjusts committee assignments so that zoning or budget decisions flow through fewer hands. Meetings still occur. Votes are still taken. But the range of outcomes quietly shrinks.

Personnel changes usually accelerate this process. Positions that once emphasized expertise begin to favor reliability and alignment. Temporary appointments linger longer than expected. Oversight roles remain unfilled through successive cycles. Experienced professionals move on quietly, taking institutional memory with them. None of this violates formal rules, but it reshapes how judgment is exercised inside the institution.

Process follows the same pattern. Timelines shorten. Review thresholds tighten. Appeals become harder to sustain. What was once discretionary becomes routine. What once raised questions becomes background. In a neighborhood planning board, this can mean public objections are technically accepted but effectively sidelined by procedural compression. Participation remains allowed, but influence weakens.

Informal pressure plays a central role. Explicit directives are rare. Instead, people learn by observing which actions create friction and which pass unnoticed. Careers stall. Budgets contract. Responsibilities shift. The lesson spreads without being stated: some choices are easier than others. Adjustment becomes a form of self-protection.

From the outside, institutions still appear intact. Cases are processed. Reports are issued. Policies are enforced—sometimes. But internally, judgment narrows. Enforcement becomes uneven. Independence survives in name, but not always in practice.

What often goes unseen is that capture does not only hollow institutions out. It also crowds out alternatives. Community media projects lose access to public information streams. Cooperative economic initiatives struggle to navigate licensing environments that have become less forgiving. Independent civic organizations remain legal but increasingly peripheral. The institutional ecosystem thins, even as its formal architecture remains standing.

This dynamic depends on ambiguity. When boundaries are unclear, hesitation replaces confidence. When consequences are unpredictable, people adapt. Authoritarian systems exploit this uncertainty not through force, but through persistence. They rely on the fact that no single decision feels decisive enough to resist.

Only a small number of people need to adjust for this process to take hold. Once they do, the institution begins to regulate itself. Resistance becomes isolated. Compliance becomes normal. And the system continues along its altered path even after public attention shifts elsewhere.

Understanding this matters because it clarifies both the risk and the opportunity. Institutions are vulnerable precisely because they depend on routine behavior. But that also means they respond to sustained, well-placed pressure. Not all at once. Not dramatically. But measurably.

The next section turns to where that pressure can still be applied—and why institutions that feel unreachable from the outside often contain points of leverage that remain accessible, especially at the local level, when participation is deliberate and sustained.

Section 3

Where Institutional Leverage Still Exists

Institutions can feel sealed off from public influence, especially once procedures become technical and decision-making retreats behind closed doors. This sense of distance is not accidental. Complexity discourages engagement, and disengagement creates room for capture. But distance is not the same as inaccessibility.

Even highly professionalized institutions depend on inputs that remain exposed. Funding streams. Appointments. Oversight mechanisms. Public legitimacy. External partnerships. These are not abstract forces. They are the points where institutional behavior intersects with the outside world—and where pressure can still register.

One source of leverage lies in visibility. Institutions rely on the assumption that most of what they do will go unnoticed. When decisions attract attention—sustained attention rather than momentary outrage—behavior changes. A school board that has grown accustomed to rubber-stamping agenda items begins to document its reasoning more carefully once meetings are regularly attended and recorded. A city council that once relied on procedural speed slows down when its voting patterns are tracked over time. Documentation starts to matter again. Justifications become more deliberate. Informal shortcuts are reconsidered.

Procedure itself is another point of leverage. Rules that can be bent can also be enforced. Requirements that are applied selectively can be applied evenly. Appeals that are discouraged can still be pursued—patiently, repeatedly, and within the system's own language. Institutions respond when the cost of ignoring their own processes begins to outweigh the cost of following them. That shift rarely comes from confrontation. It comes from persistence.

Professional norms also exert pressure, often more quietly than public criticism. Many people inside institutions care deeply about standards, reputation, and legitimacy within their field. When decisions begin to conflict with those norms, discomfort spreads—even among those who would not describe themselves as political. A regulatory office that suddenly attracts scrutiny from peer organizations, accrediting bodies, or professional associations may begin to adjust behavior without any public clash. External engagement that is informed and precise can amplify this tension without turning it into spectacle.

There is leverage, too, in relationships institutions rely on to function. Public agencies partner with community organizations. School districts depend on cooperation from parents, educators, and local nonprofits. Local governments rely on media, vendors, and civic groups to carry out everyday work. When those relationships become conditional—when legitimacy can no longer be assumed—institutions feel constraint even if formal authority remains unchanged.

Time itself is another pressure point. Authoritarian systems rely on speed and fatigue. Institutions move more slowly by design. When participation is patient rather than reactive, it can exploit that difference. Reviews matter. Delays matter. Waiting out a news cycle does not neutralize pressure that persists beyond it.

What makes these forms of leverage effective is coordination. Isolated complaints are easy to dismiss. Patterned engagement is harder to ignore. When multiple actors return to the same meeting, the same office, or the same decision over time, institutions begin to feel bounded again—not because they are threatened, but because their operating environment has changed.

This kind of pressure is rarely satisfying in the short term. It produces few dramatic moments. But it accumulates. It restores friction in systems that depend on smooth operation to consolidate power. And over time, that friction can make the difference between institutions that continue to bend—and institutions that begin, quietly, to hold.

The next section looks at how this pressure can be sustained without exhausting the people applying it. How institutional engagement can fit into ordinary life rather than demand constant vigilance. And why endurance, not intensity, is what ultimately determines whether leverage remains possible at all.

Section 4
Designing Institutional Engagement for Endurance

Sustained institutional pressure often fails for the same reason many resistance efforts fail: it asks too much, too often, from too few people. Following procedures, tracking decisions, filing challenges, and maintaining oversight are cognitively demanding and emotionally unrewarding forms of work. When engagement is designed as constant vigilance, burnout is almost inevitable.

Endurance requires a different approach. Institutional engagement has to be shaped so it can exist alongside ordinary life. That means narrowing scope, clarifying responsibility, and accepting that no one can watch everything all the time. What matters is not total coverage, but continuity.

In practice, this often looks less dramatic than people expect. A small group of residents may decide to consistently attend school board meetings—not to intervene every time, but to listen, record, and notice patterns. Over time, familiarity builds. Deviations become easier to spot. Questions become more precise. The institution adjusts, not because it is confronted, but because it is no longer operating unseen.

Role distribution is another quiet stabilizer. Instead of asking individuals to monitor entire systems, responsibility is divided into manageable portions. One set of people follows appointments and resignations. Another tracks rule changes and meeting agendas. Another pays attention to enforcement outcomes rather than policy language. Each role is limited enough to be sustainable, but connected enough to matter when patterns emerge.

Durable engagement also depends on shared memory. Institutions often outlast public attention because they rely on forgetting. When participants cycle in and out without continuity, lessons are lost and effort resets. In contrast, even informal records—notes from meetings, timelines of decisions, recollections of how processes used to function—can anchor collective understanding. This is not about creating experts. It is about preventing erosion from proceeding unchecked simply because no one remembers what "normal" once looked like.

Pacing plays a role as well. Institutional work unfolds slowly, and pressure that mirrors that pace is often more effective than urgency that burns out quickly. When engagement follows a rhythm—returning monthly, reviewing quarterly, following up annually—it becomes part of the environment rather than an interruption. Institutions learn that attention will return. Waiting out a news cycle no longer resolves the issue.

Restraint is equally important. Not every decision requires response. Not every deviation warrants escalation. Strategic patience allows people to conserve energy and choose moments that matter most. This selectivity is not passivity. It is how pressure remains credible rather than performative.

Most importantly, engagement becomes sustainable when absence does not equal collapse. When someone steps back, others can carry the work forward temporarily. When responsibility is shared, participation can stretch across changes in capacity, interest, and circumstance. This flexibility is what allows institutional pressure to persist through years rather than weeks.

The final section of this chapter brings these strands together. It looks at how institutional engagement fits within the broader democratic strategy developed throughout the book—not as a replacement for public action or electoral politics, but as the connective tissue that allows those efforts to accumulate rather than dissipate.

Section 5

Institutions as the Line That Holds

Institutions are rarely where democratic movements begin. They are too slow, too technical, and too removed from everyday experience to inspire mass engagement. But they are often where democratic survival is decided.

When institutions hold, they slow consolidation. They introduce friction. They create delays that matter. They preserve space for participation to recover when public attention wanes. Even imperfectly functioning institutions can buy time, and time is one of the most underappreciated resources in democratic defense.

This is visible in moments that rarely make headlines. A court that insists on procedure even when pressure mounts. A regulatory body that delays implementation long enough for scrutiny to return. A local board that refuses to waive requirements simply because it would be more convenient to do so. None of these actions feel decisive in isolation. But together, they prevent erosion from becoming irreversible.

This is why institutional engagement should not be treated as a specialized concern or a fallback strategy. It is part of the core architecture that allows other forms of resistance to work. Public protest draws attention. Electoral participation changes leadership. Narrative work shapes legitimacy. Institutional pressure ensures that none of those efforts evaporate once the moment passes.

Authoritarian systems understand this connection clearly. They do not attack institutions because institutions are symbolic. They attack them because institutions constrain power in ways that are difficult to reverse once lost. When courts, regulators, and administrative bodies no longer operate independently, democratic action becomes episodic rather than cumulative. Each effort has to start from zero again.

The work described in this chapter is not dramatic, and it is not heroic. It does not produce immediate victories or visible turning points. Its value lies in persistence —in maintaining standards when it would be easier to adapt, in following procedures when others hope no one will, and in showing up again after attention has shifted elsewhere.

This kind of engagement does not require large numbers of people. It requires enough people, acting deliberately, to change the conditions under which decisions are made. When institutional pressure is steady, even concentrated power has to account for it. When it disappears, erosion accelerates.

What ultimately makes institutions defensible is not their design alone, but the environment around them. Institutions reflect the level of engagement that surrounds them. When scrutiny fades, discretion expands. When attention returns, limits reappear.

This is the connective logic of democratic endurance. Institutions do not save democracy on their own. But without them, other forms of resistance struggle to accumulate. They are the line that holds long enough for participation to matter again.

The next chapter shifts focus once more—from institutions back to people. Specifically, to how democratic participation is sustained across disagreement, fatigue, and slow progress. Because defending democracy is not only about stopping erosion. It is about building habits of engagement that can survive long after crisis no longer feels urgent.

Section 6

What This Looks Like

Local power building rarely looks like power at first. It looks like paperwork. Agendas. Minutes. Committee assignments. An unusual delay. A rule that used to be applied one way and is now applied another.

For most people, the first sign of institutional change is not a headline. It's a small friction in ordinary life: a request that used to be straightforward becomes complicated; a decision that once took weeks now stalls for months; a public process feels suddenly opaque. Taken alone, these moments feel like inefficiency. Over time, they begin to feel like pattern.

Institutional engagement that endures begins when someone treats those patterns as readable. Not dramatic, not conspiratorial—just legible. People start attending a meeting not because they expect a turning point, but because they want to understand how decisions are being routed. They begin to recognize what "normal" looks like inside that room: who speaks, who defers, what gets moved quickly, what is never discussed, which questions are answered and which are redirected.

Nothing about this feels heroic. It often feels dull. But the dullness is part of the leverage. Institutions rely on the assumption that complexity and boredom will keep scrutiny away. When a small number of people return consistently—without rage, without theatrics—the operating environment changes. Justifications become more careful. Process becomes more visible. Shortcuts are used less casually. Not because the institution has been defeated, but because it is no longer unobserved.

What makes this sustainable is not intensity, but distribution. One person can't track everything and shouldn't try. A small group remains effective by dividing attention into narrow, repeatable roles: one follows agendas and procedural changes, another tracks appointments and resignations, another notices enforcement patterns, another keeps memory of how things used to work. Each role is limited enough to coexist with ordinary life. Together, they create continuity.

A key feature of local leverage is that it often shows up as restraint. People learn not to challenge every decision, not to treat every meeting as a confrontation. Instead, they notice when something matters—when a procedure is being rewritten, when oversight is being narrowed, when independence is being tested—and they return to the same point repeatedly, calmly, over time. That repetition signals something institutions understand: this will not disappear after a news cycle.

Institutional pressure also becomes real when it is translated into professional language. Not because citizens must become experts, but because systems respond to their own standards. A well-formed question, asked again and again, forces documentation. Documentation forces consistency. Consistency restores limits. This is slow work, but it is cumulative work—the kind that prevents erosion from becoming normalized simply because no one can point to where it happened.

Over time, the most important change is psychological. Institutions stop feeling unreachable. People begin to understand that influence is not a single moment of victory. It is the gradual restoration of friction: slowing decisions that assume automatic passage, increasing the cost of selective enforcement, making informal pressure less effective because it is noticed.

This is what it means for institutions to become the line that holds. Not through dramatic confrontation, but through sustained presence that makes quiet bending harder to sustain. When institutions are watched over time, they are less able to drift without explanation. When procedures are followed persistently, discretion narrows. When memory is preserved, normalization becomes harder.

And this is where local power building fits the larger design of the book. It does not demand constant vigilance. It turns vigilance into rhythm. It does not require everyone. It requires enough people, returning reliably, to keep democratic limits from dissolving into habit.

The next chapter returns to the human problem underneath all of this: how participation survives disagreement, fatigue, and slow progress—so that the work of holding institutions does not collapse into the very burnout authoritarian systems depend on.

CHAPTER 11
Measuring and Building Victory

Section 1

Why "Winning" Is the Wrong Question

People often ask whether democratic efforts are *working* as if progress should announce itself clearly. Did the policy pass. Did the election flip. Did the movement win. These questions make sense, but they are poorly suited to the kind of struggle this book has been describing. They assume that change arrives as a visible outcome, at a recognizable moment, with a clear before and after.

Democratic erosion does not happen that way. And democratic recovery rarely does either.

Authoritarian systems consolidate gradually, through accumulation rather than rupture. Power shifts first in procedures, then in expectations, then in habits. By the time outcomes are unmistakable, the conditions that produced them have been in place for years. Measuring democratic defense by headline victories misunderstands the terrain. It looks for confirmation where confirmation is least likely to appear.

This is why "winning" is the wrong organizing question.

The more useful question is whether conditions are changing in ways that make further erosion harder and collective action easier. Whether decisions are encountering friction again. Whether institutions hesitate where they once moved freely. Whether people who had withdrawn begin to reappear—not dramatically, but reliably. These shifts are subtle, and they are easy to miss if you are only watching for decisive moments.

Authoritarian systems depend on people believing that nothing short of total reversal matters. That belief accelerates withdrawal. If progress must be obvious to count, then slow gains feel like failure. Fatigue follows. Engagement thins. The system benefits from that disappointment, because it thrives when people stop noticing incremental constraint.

Democratic endurance requires a different orientation. It treats progress as cumulative rather than conclusive. It pays attention to capacity instead of climax. It asks whether participation is becoming easier to sustain, whether pressure is becoming harder to ignore, and whether adaptation is becoming less comfortable for those consolidating power.

This does not mean abandoning the hope of outcomes. It means understanding their timing. Outcomes arrive after conditions have shifted, not before. They are the visible effects of quieter work that has already altered incentives, expectations, and limits.

This chapter is about learning how to recognize those quieter signals without needing constant reassurance. Not to lower standards. Not to rationalize stagnation. But to stay oriented when progress does not announce itself loudly or quickly.

Because the work described in this book is not designed to produce a single moment of victory. It is designed to change what happens next—and what becomes possible after that.

Section 2

What Endurance Actually Looks Like

Endurance is often misunderstood as stubbornness or sheer willpower. As if democratic participation succeeds because people simply try harder, stay angrier longer, or refuse to give up. That misunderstanding is one of the reasons so many well-intentioned efforts collapse. Endurance is not a personality trait. It is an environmental outcome.

People persist when engagement fits into their lives without requiring constant sacrifice. They persist when effort feels shared rather than isolating. They persist when participation produces some sense of continuity—even when progress is slow or invisible. When those conditions are absent, no amount of conviction compensates for exhaustion.

In authoritarian systems, endurance is engineered from above. Compliance is routinized. Dissent is made costly. Withdrawal is rewarded with quiet relief. Democratic endurance has to be engineered differently. It cannot rely on fear, obligation, or loyalty tests. It has to rely on habit.

Habit is less dramatic than mobilization, but far more powerful over time. Habits do not require constant decision-making. They reduce friction. They allow participation to continue even when motivation dips or attention drifts. This is why democratic work that survives rarely looks heroic. It looks repetitive. Predictable. Sometimes dull.

Endurance also depends on expectation management. People burn out fastest when they believe engagement should produce immediate transformation. When reality fails to meet that expectation, discouragement sets in. Sustainable participation requires a more accurate sense of scale. Most democratic defense does not reverse damage quickly. It slows it. It complicates it. It raises costs. These effects are cumulative, but they are rarely satisfying in isolation.

Another feature of endurance is reversibility. People need to be able to step back temporarily without feeling they have abandoned the cause or let others down. Systems that punish absence eventually drive people away. Systems that absorb absence allow people to return. This flexibility is not a weakness. It is how participation survives changing life circumstances.

Endurance also looks uneven. Some periods demand more attention. Others recede into maintenance. There are moments of visibility and long stretches of quiet work. Expecting constant intensity misunderstands how democratic pressure actually accumulates. What matters is not how loudly people show up at any given moment, but whether engagement remains possible across time.

Seen this way, endurance is not about holding on at all costs. It is about designing participation so that holding on does not feel like a cost in the first place. When engagement becomes livable, people stop measuring their involvement by how much they can sacrifice and start measuring it by how long they can stay.

The next section turns to what sustains that livability over years rather than months. Not motivation. Not outrage. But the social and structural conditions that allow people to remain engaged even when results are partial, delayed, or difficult to see.

Section 3

Staying Engaged Across Differences

One of the quietest threats to democratic endurance is not repression or exhaustion, but fracture. Participation often falters not because people stop caring, but because disagreement becomes intolerable. When every difference is treated as a threat, movements narrow. When belonging depends on alignment, participation becomes fragile.

Democracy, by definition, involves sustained disagreement. It requires people to work alongside others who share goals but not priorities, language, or temperament. That tension is not a flaw in democratic participation. It is a condition of it. Endurance depends on whether movements can absorb disagreement without turning it into exit.

Authoritarian systems solve this problem by eliminating ambiguity. Loyalty substitutes for trust. Unity is enforced rather than negotiated. Democratic systems cannot—and should not—replicate that approach. They have to build endurance in a more difficult way: by normalizing difference without letting it dissolve shared purpose.

This begins with expectations. Democratic participation often falters when people assume agreement should come easily, or that conflict signals failure. In reality, disagreement is evidence of engagement. What matters is not whether conflict arises, but whether it is contained in ways that allow work to continue.

Enduring movements develop informal norms that make disagreement survivable. Arguments do not automatically become moral verdicts. Mistakes do not become permanent identities. People are allowed to revise their views without humiliation. These norms are rarely written down, but they shape whether people stay.

Another element is role differentiation. When participation is narrowly defined, disagreement feels existential. If there is only one way to belong, any conflict threatens expulsion. When participation takes multiple forms, people can continue contributing even when they disagree about direction, emphasis, or timing. This flexibility allows movements to retain people rather than force constant sorting.

Endurance also requires restraint in moments of tension. Not every disagreement needs resolution. Not every internal conflict needs public performance. Sometimes the most durable choice is to let disagreement remain unresolved while work continues elsewhere. This is not avoidance. It is prioritization.

Importantly, staying engaged across difference does not mean tolerating everything. Democratic participation still requires boundaries—around good faith, shared purpose, and basic respect. Endurance depends on knowing which lines protect the work and which merely narrow it.

Movements that survive over time do not eliminate conflict. They make it less destabilizing. They create conditions in which disagreement does not automatically trigger withdrawal or escalation. That stability allows people to remain engaged even when consensus is incomplete.

The next section turns to one final condition of endurance: how participation is renewed across generations and life stages, rather than concentrated in a single cohort that eventually exhausts itself. Because democratic work does not only need persistence—it needs continuity.

Section 4

Renewing Participation Over Time

Democratic participation often concentrates among the same people, at the same moments, for the same reasons. Crises activate engagement. Urgency pulls people in. And then—gradually—life intervenes. Careers shift. Families change. Energy fades. Without renewal, even the most committed movements thin out.

Authoritarian systems benefit from this pattern. They do not need to eliminate participation entirely. They only need to wait for it to age out. When resistance is built around a fixed cohort, endurance becomes a race against time.

Renewal requires designing participation that can be entered and exited without collapse. People should be able to step back during demanding periods of life and return later without penalty or loss of belonging. When engagement assumes constant availability, it silently excludes anyone whose circumstances change.

This is especially true across generations. Younger participants often bring urgency, creativity, and risk tolerance. Older participants bring memory, institutional knowledge, and strategic patience. Movements weaken when these strengths are separated or treated as competing cultures rather than complementary ones.

Continuity emerges when roles are designed to shift with capacity. Someone who organizes intensively at one stage of life may later mentor, advise, document, or support behind the scenes. Another person may enter with limited involvement and grow into leadership over time. Endurance depends on these transitions being normal rather than exceptional.

Memory also plays a role. Democratic participation is often forced to relearn lessons because experience leaves with individuals. Renewal that discards institutional memory wastes effort and repeats mistakes. Movements that endure find ways to preserve context without rigid hierarchy—through shared narratives, informal mentorship, and accessible records of what has been tried before.

Importantly, renewal does not mean constant expansion. It means maintaining permeability. New participants can enter without displacing those already involved. Longtime contributors can shift roles without disappearing. Participation remains open rather than brittle.

When renewal works, engagement stops feeling like a finite sprint and starts feeling like a rhythm. People move in and out, but the work continues. That continuity is difficult to see in the moment, but it is one of the clearest markers of democratic endurance.

The final section brings these strands together. It returns to the central question this book has asked throughout: not how to win quickly, but how to remain engaged long enough for democratic constraints to reassert themselves—without burning out the people who sustain them.

Section 5

Staying Engaged When Progress Is Slow

One of the hardest truths about democratic work is that success rarely feels like success while it is happening. Progress is uneven. Gains are partial. Setbacks recur. Long stretches pass with no visible improvement at all. For many people, this is where engagement quietly dissolves.

Authoritarian systems exploit this gap between effort and reward. They promise decisiveness. They dramatize action. They frame complexity as failure. When democratic work feels slow by comparison, it can begin to feel ineffective—even when it is doing exactly what it must do.

The danger here is not disappointment. It is misinterpretation. Slow progress is often mistaken for lack of impact, when in fact it may indicate that resistance is imposing friction. Delays, reversals, procedural obstacles, and narrowed options are rarely celebrated, but they are signs that consolidation is no longer effortless.

Sustaining engagement under these conditions requires a shift in how success is understood. Instead of measuring progress by visible victories, democratic endurance depends on recognizing prevented harms, stalled abuses, and preserved space. These outcomes are harder to point to, but they are no less real.

People stay engaged when effort feels meaningful, even if it is not immediately gratifying. That meaning comes from clarity of purpose and connection to others doing parallel work. When individuals can see how their contribution fits into a larger pattern, patience becomes more tolerable.

Another factor is honesty about time horizons. Democratic repair does not move at the speed of outrage. It unfolds through accumulation—of pressure, of participation, of institutional memory. When movements acknowledge this openly, they reduce the sense of personal failure that often accompanies slow change.

Staying engaged also requires permission to feel frustration without converting it into withdrawal. Disappointment does not mean disengagement is the right response. It often means expectations need recalibration. Endurance is not the absence of frustration. It is the ability to continue despite it.

What ultimately sustains participation during slow periods is shared rhythm. Regular touchpoints. Familiar practices. Predictable forms of contribution. These create a sense of motion even when outcomes lag. People are more likely to stay when engagement is woven into life rather than treated as a constant emergency.

This is where democratic work begins to resemble stewardship rather than struggle. The task is not to force resolution, but to maintain conditions in which resolution remains possible. That orientation does not produce dramatic moments, but it does produce continuity.

The concluding section turns to that orientation directly. It reflects on what it means to live inside democratic responsibility without constant crisis, and how engagement becomes something people can carry forward—not as a reaction to threat, but as an ongoing practice.

Section 6

Carrying Democratic Responsibility Forward

If democracy is to endure, engagement cannot remain tied only to moments of threat. Crisis can awaken participation, but it cannot sustain it indefinitely. When engagement depends on alarm, it becomes exhausting. When it depends on outrage, it becomes brittle. What lasts is something quieter and more ordinary.

Democratic responsibility, at its core, is not a stance taken once and held forever. It is a practice that unfolds over time. People enter it at different moments, with different capacities, and for different reasons. Some arrive through anger. Others through concern. Many through necessity. What matters is not how participation begins, but whether it can continue without consuming everything else.

This is why the book has emphasized design over intensity at every stage. Systems that endure are not those that demand constant sacrifice. They are those that allow people to contribute without disappearing into the work. Engagement that can be carried forward must coexist with family, employment, disagreement, and fatigue. It must leave room for life.

Carrying responsibility forward also means releasing the idea that democracy is defended by heroes. That story flatters a few and discourages the rest. In reality, democratic survival has always depended on ordinary people doing unremarkable things consistently. Showing up to meetings. Asking procedural questions. Voting in low-turnout elections. Following up when others hope attention has moved on. These actions rarely feel historic. Their power lies in repetition.

Another shift involves how identity relates to engagement. When participation becomes a measure of moral worth, it fractures quickly. People withdraw rather than risk failure. Sustainable engagement treats participation as contribution, not as proof. It allows people to step back and return. It recognizes effort without demanding permanence.

Over time, this approach changes how democracy is experienced. Instead of something that is defended only when it is threatened, it becomes something that is maintained. Instead of a constant struggle, it becomes a shared responsibility. That shift does not eliminate conflict or disagreement. It makes them survivable.

What this book has traced, chapter by chapter, is a path away from reactive resistance and toward democratic endurance. From understanding how erosion happens, to learning from failed movements, to designing participation that can persist. None of this offers certainty. Democracy has never come with guarantees. What it offers instead is possibility—conditional on engagement that lasts longer than any single crisis.

The work does not end when attention fades or headlines change. In many ways, that is when it truly begins. Democracy is preserved not in moments of clarity, but in long stretches of ambiguity. Not by intensity, but by continuity.

This is the final invitation of the book. Not to remain permanently alarmed. Not to take on more than you can carry. But to find a form of engagement that fits into your life and stays there. Because authoritarian systems advance when people withdraw. Democratic systems survive when participation becomes ordinary again.

Section 7

What This Looks Like

By the time people reach the end of this book, many are still quietly waiting for something that feels like confirmation. Some sign that the work is paying off. Some marker that effort has translated into progress in a way that can be clearly named.

But democratic defense rarely offers that kind of reassurance. The changes that matter most tend to arrive before there is anything obvious to celebrate. They show up not as victories, but as resistance to inevitability—small interruptions in what had begun to move too easily.

In practice, one of the first signs that conditions are shifting is friction. Decisions that once moved smoothly begin to slow. Processes that were treated as formalities require justification again. Institutions that had grown accustomed to operating without scrutiny start documenting their reasoning more carefully. Nothing dramatic has happened, and yet something has changed: power is no longer moving without cost.

This kind of friction is easy to misinterpret. It does not feel like progress. It feels like inconvenience, delay, inefficiency. But inefficiency is precisely what authoritarian consolidation seeks to eliminate. Smoothness is not neutrality; it is a condition of unchecked power. When systems become less smooth, less predictable, and less insulated from attention, democratic constraint is quietly reasserting itself.

Another signal appears in return. Not mass mobilization or sudden enthusiasm, but the steady reappearance of people who had previously withdrawn. They show up not only at moments of crisis, but in ordinary settings—local meetings, administrative hearings, school boards, neighborhood associations. Participation does not surge; it resumes. And that resumption matters more than intensity ever could, because authoritarian systems rely on disengagement remaining permanent.

Return also changes the tone of public life. Fatalism softens. Conversations shift from abstract despair toward concrete questions: what can be done here, now, within reach. When participation becomes practical again, it no longer needs to be dramatic to feel worthwhile.

Memory is another quiet indicator. Power consolidates most easily where attention resets repeatedly, where each new controversy erases the last, and where people are forced to relearn the same lessons again and again. Democratic endurance begins to accumulate when memory holds—through shared records, consistent language, repeated reference points, and people who can say, calmly and accurately, how things used to work and how they changed. When forgetting becomes harder, normalization loses its grip.

Over time, this memory supports role stability. Engagement stops depending on constant improvisation and emotional urgency. Instead, it settles into recognizable forms of contribution—people who track decisions, follow procedures, document patterns, maintain continuity, and return reliably. These roles are not glamorous, but they are sustainable. They allow participation to persist even when motivation fluctuates, because habit replaces constant choice.

Coalitions also begin to change. Movements that measure success only by agreement tend to fracture quickly, narrowing until they become brittle. Enduring democratic efforts look different. They survive disagreement without turning every difference into a test of belonging. They allow people to remain engaged even when consensus is incomplete. This capacity to absorb tension without collapse is one of the clearest signs that participation is becoming livable again.

As these conditions develop, neutrality starts to carry a different weight. Authoritarian systems depend on accommodation feeling safe and withdrawal feeling rational. Democratic pressure becomes real when that calculation begins to shift—when institutions, organizations, and individuals discover that silence now invites scrutiny rather than protection, and that procedural deflection no longer ends the conversation. This does not require punishment or spectacle. It emerges through consistency, visibility, and return.

Taken together, these changes are easy to miss if you are only looking for victory. They do not resolve conflict. They do not close the story. What they do is alter the background conditions under which power operates. They make further erosion harder, more expensive, and less automatic.

This is why "winning" is the wrong measure. If progress must announce itself clearly in order to count, people will withdraw precisely when their effort is beginning to matter. Authoritarian systems benefit from that disappointment, because they depend on people believing that nothing short of total reversal is meaningful.

The alternative is not to lower expectations, but to measure the right things: whether decisions encounter resistance again; whether institutions hesitate where they once moved freely; whether participation is becoming repeatable rather than exceptional; whether memory is accumulating instead of resetting; whether disagreement is survivable; whether withdrawal is no longer the easiest option.

When enough of these conditions shift, outcomes become more likely—not guaranteed, but possible—because the terrain has changed. Democratic repair begins long before it becomes visible.

This is the orientation the book ultimately asks you to adopt. Not permanent alarm. Not heroic sacrifice. But durability. A form of engagement that fits into your life and stays there, even when results are partial and progress is slow.

Democracy has never been preserved by people who waited for certainty. It has been preserved by people who returned. Again and again. Quietly. Not because they felt inspired, but because they refused to let withdrawal become normal.

That is what victory looks like in real time: not a moment of triumph, but the restoration of constraint—enough friction, enough participation, enough continuity—to keep power from consolidating smoothly. Not an ending. A change in what happens next.

MEASURING AND BUILDING VICTORY

THE END